A GARDENER'S GUIDE TO
BIOLOGICAL PEST CONTROL

Using natural predators in the garden

To Anna,

Not quite bed time reading
but hope you enjoy!

Love,
Jules

A GARDENER'S GUIDE TO
BIOLOGICAL PEST CONTROL

Using natural predators in the garden

JULIAN IVES

THE CROWOOD PRESS

First published in 2022 by
The Crowood Press Ltd
Ramsbury, Marlborough
Wiltshire SN8 2HR

enquiries@crowood.com

www.crowood.com

British Library Cataloguing-in-Publication Data
A catalogue record for this book is available from the British Library.

ISBN 978 0 7198 4094 4

Front cover image: Ger Bosma
Photos/Shutterstock.com

Back cover soft scale insect and lacewing larvae
Photos: Koppert Biological Systems

Typeset by Chennai Publishing Services
Cover design by Blue Sunflower Creative
Printed and bound in India by Parksons Graphics Pvt Ltd

CONTENTS

INTRODUCTION

The future of garden pest control will increasingly rely on the use of their natural enemies to combat a wide range of garden pest invaders. This is not a newly discovered method of pest control, however, and examples of early biological control can be traced back centuries. Applications of biological control were used in Ancient Egypt and China, for instance, where cats were often introduced to control rats. The now widespread use of biological control can be credited to more recent developments in food production and horticulture, where it is commonly referred to as biological pest control. The terminology can be more accurately defined as the suppression and control of unwanted insects through the introduction of their natural enemies. These enemies may be in the form of predators, parasites or other organisms.

The Downfall of Insecticides

Throughout the twentieth century, insect pest control largely relied on the use of insecticides. These insecticides were relatively cheap to produce and easily accessible. They were used on a vast scale with frequent repeat applications. The issue in using man-made insecticides and pesticides, however, is that insects adapt. Each time a chemical application is made, a small number of the target insects survive, and if the same insecticide is used repeatedly, this percentage rises. This creates a necessity for pesticides to contain new active ingredients to combat the increasing insect resistance. New active ingredients require more chemistry and the cost of finding and producing these new products becomes more expensive. This has been compounded by rising registration costs for agrochemical companies. These costs are due to government charges for pesticides to be tested prior to use and sale in particular countries. Without these registrations, the products cannot legally be sold or applied. The impact of all these costs is that fewer new insecticides become available to the market. It is right, however, that these pesticides are vigorously tested, as many pesticides have proven over time to be harmful to the environment. It is these environmental concerns, costs and pressures that have helped to stimulate the increased use of biological and natural pest control.

There has also been pressure from consumers wishing to use organic or pesticide-free produce. This has led to the establishment of maximum residue levels (MRLs) permitted on produce. These rules are set by governments. Retailers such as supermarkets are now required to check that their produce conforms to these standards. This has forced the growers of produce to explore chemical-free methods of producing food. Biological control of insect pests in the production of crops, grown under glass or in protected areas, is now standard procedure. Crops, such as tomatoes, cucumbers and peppers, and soft fruit, such as strawberries, now have natural enemies introduced to them on a regular basis. This has led to a significant expansion in the number of commercially reared insects for pest control. Natural enemies are now frequently produced to control numerous and varying pests. Commercial growers have also learnt how to use these natural enemies and some of this knowledge will be passed on in this book.

The Impact of Bees

Bees are highly valued insects, typically for their powers of pollination. It was the introduction of bumblebees to tomato greenhouses, however, that also led to another surge in the use of natural enemies. Bumblebees are fantastic pollinators and growers quickly recognized their value in increasing yields. One side effect of their introduction was that insecticides could not be used in greenhouses where bumblebees were at work. Growers therefore became increasingly favourable to pesticide-free control methods, most notably by using the natural enemies of pests. Using bumblebees for pollination therefore encouraged growers to innovate new methods of insect pest control that would avoid using harmful insecticides. These natural enemies work alongside the bumblebees to protect the plants, are safe for the environment and are harmless to the applicator. This ensures a complete natural solution to pest control and the pollination of plants.

Biological Pest Control in Gardens

It is not only professional growers that are now using biological pest control, but increasingly professional gardeners and institutions, too. The Royal Horticultural Society (RHS), for example, encourages the use of natural enemies in its own gardens and provides information via its website on how and where to source them (*see* Bibliography at the end of the book).

The National Trust and English Heritage are two further notable professional advocates that prefer the use of natural enemies wherever possible for insect pest control on their sites. These sites also increasingly promote the use of natural enemies to their visitors. Many esteemed and prestigious botanical gardens are

Thanet Earth Glasshouses, Kent. One of the leading tomato growers in the UK, they use bumblebees for pollination and biological control, and natural enemies for pest control.

The Great House at the National Botanic Garden of Wales, where predators and parasites are used for pest control.

also playing a vital role in teaching the hobby gardener how to implement this form of pest control. Botanical gardens across the UK are using natural enemies and developing new methods of utilizing these insects on their varied and large plant collections. Visitors can witness and discuss these methods when they visit the botanical gardens in Cambridge, Edinburgh, Kew and the National Botanic Garden of Wales. Gardeners are often strongly influenced by what they read, and indeed view, of actions taking place in the gardens of influential institutions and will often try to replicate such new methods in their own gardens.

Amateur or hobby gardeners are generally conscientiously eager to reduce the use of pesticides due to environmental concerns, but additionally because there may be few alternative forms of pest control. Many garden insecticides have been withdrawn from sale to consumers over the last few years, leaving some garden pests without a chemical insecticide-based solution. This has forced gardeners to look for other ways of controlling pests in their gardens. Hobby gardeners can now access biological control products more easily and quickly, predominantly through online platforms which are ideally suited to sending live material quickly through postal and courier services. Increasing information on the use of natural enemies is available online, or by visiting a professional garden that uses biological control. The benefits are abundant, combining environmentally friendly practices, which are better and safer for the planet and user, with effective pest control for the garden.

This Book

This book will offer a step-by-step guide to how, and which, natural enemies can be used in the garden to protect plants from garden pests. The book will take you from: where to start; the different natural enemies available; how to apply the enemies; the different pests you may encounter in various parts of the garden; and other tools you can use to maximize your chances of controlling insect garden pests, safely, naturally and effectively.

CHAPTER 1

WHERE TO START

There are some basic parameters that should be adhered to in deciding where and when to apply biological pest control in the garden. Many of the controls are living organisms and require certain conditions to survive and to be active. Certain organisms also have limited lifespans, so the timing of their introduction can be critical. One must also consider the size of the area requiring treatment compared with how large the pest infestation is, in order to achieve successful control. It can also take a bit longer to notice results than it would through traditional insecticide treatment, where you might see dead pest insects within a few hours of application. The biological control process is generally a longer one, often involving more frequent applications.

Certain insecticides may have an impact on several pest species, but biological control tends to be more specific. Using biological control is certainly better for the environment in this respect, as it does not cause any collateral damage to other insect species and wildlife. The biological control process simply requires more planning, which will be explained throughout this chapter.

Creating the Environment

A good starting point when switching to more natural forms of pest control, especially those reliant on the use of beneficial insects, or, as they are referred to in this book, 'natural enemies', is to create an environment in which they can survive and thrive. Certain natural enemies not only feed on pests, but can also survive on, or supplement their diet with, pollen or nectar. This means that your choice of plants can have a large influence on whether you will attract natural enemies into your garden from the wild. If you decide to introduce natural enemies, plant choice will also affect how well their populations will develop and persist. Wildflowers are generally a good source of pollen and nectar, as are some trees and shrubs. Fennel, dill, sunflowers and even dandelions will provide a good source of pollen and nectar for lacewings, a highly beneficial insect. Marigolds, tansy and common yarrow will help to attract ladybirds, another beneficial insect. A suitable all-rounder shrub for many beneficial insects is the buddleia.

A neat and manicured lawn may look smart, but it provides extraordinarily little in the way of useful habitat for natural enemies. This can be offset by stocking the borders around the lawn with pollen and nectar-bearing plants. Some local authorities are also changing their planting schemes, moving away from traditional bedding plants, which often produce less pollen and nectar than wildflowers. This is occurring in Harrogate, for example, where the famous Stray is being partially planted with wildflowers instead of

Wildflowers and grasses on Harrogate Stray. A good example of where consideration has been made by the local council to establish plants that will attract beneficial insects.

bedding plants. There have also been some developments with seed companies that now sell predator-friendly seed mixes.

Some plants that may not be on a gardener's first-choice list can also provide useful habitats or staging posts for predators and parasites of insect pests. For example, if you look at nettles and thistles in the summer, they are often alive with insects. Many of these plants host predators of aphids, such as ladybird larvae, and even mummified aphids, which have been parasitized by aphid parasites. Such plants are often known as 'banker plants', as they accumulate populations of natural enemies that will migrate on to plants around them that are riddled with pests. Leaving a corner or small area in the garden with a few nettles or flowering thistles can pay dividends in terms of free natural pest control.

Many gardeners, when designing their gardens, will attempt to have certain plants in flower at different times for appearance, but this will also provide a constant source of pollen and nectar, which is helpful in maintaining beneficial insect levels. When planning a design, it is sensible to check that the varieties you are considering are also good sources of pollen and nectar.

To encourage certain natural enemies, for example ladybirds, to stay in your garden over the winter months, an artificial habitat such as a log pile can be created. No specific design is required, but ensure that it is large enough to create the cracks and crevices that ladybirds like to overwinter in as adults. This is often represented in a domestic setting when ladybird adults are found in window frames as you open them up in the spring. Log piles will also provide an ideal overwintering site for other beneficial insects, such as lacewings. Insect habitats or 'hotels' are also available online, or in garden centres. Some of these 'hotels' are a bit misleading, however, as they are often portrayed as places where insects 'check in and out' on a regular basis throughout the year, and this is not how they work.

The occupation of insects will often depend on where you place the habitats. One of the more successful types of insect hotels are those used for attracting solitary bees. If you position these hotels in a south to south-east facing direction in a garden

Ladybirds feasting on aphids.

A mason bee preparing to lay eggs in nesting tubes. Multiple eggs develop inside these tubes, which are then sealed at the end by the bee with soil and clay.
I. ROTTLAENDER/SHUTTERSTOCK.COM

Log pile. A log pile provides a good location for beneficial insects to hide and overwinter.

with pollen-bearing plants, you will often find their tube ends sealed with sand or soil, which indicates that several solitary bee cocoons are developing inside. These cocoons will mature over a year and bees will hatch from the tubes in the spring, providing a source of natural pollinators for your garden. If you position these hotels facing north, they will remain vacant and empty, as indeed will other insect hotels in gardens that have no pollen- or nectar-bearing plants. Log piles or discarded leaf litter will also sometimes provide a home for roving beetles, which can feed on a variety of garden pests including small slugs.

Climate and Temperatures

Climate and fluctuating temperatures have a huge influence on pests and their natural enemies. Mild winters will often lead to higher pest populations in the spring, as many are not killed off by normal patterns of colder temperatures. Global warming is making these occurrences more frequent and is helping to create the conditions for more non-native pests to establish in areas not previously observed. This creates more challenges for the gardener, as initially no native predators are present. Nature adapts, however, and an example of such adaptation is found with the horse-chestnut leaf miner (*Cameraria ohridella*). This is a recent invader from foreign shores, which has become an established pest of many horse-chestnut trees. If you look closely, however, you will often see large populations of blue tits feeding on them. These birds have adapted to a new food supply provided by the horse-chestnut leaf miners (*see* Chapter 9 for more information on horse-chestnut leaf miners).

Temperature has a direct impact on pest development and indeed the development of their natural enemies. To achieve success with biological control, it is imperative to make sure that conditions are warm enough for natural enemies to be active.

Some pests, however, can become active before their predators or parasites. This is exemplified by whitefly and aphids, which can survive and reproduce at quite low temperatures. This is often identified in vacant greenhouses during winter where weeds have been left. These conditions are all that is required to provide an overwintering site for whitefly or aphids. Once the greenhouse is utilized again in the spring,

Leaf miner mines showing on horse-chestnut leaves. The tiny moths lay eggs that develop into larvae, which tunnel into the leaves.

the pests simply transfer to newly propagated plants. It is not possible to introduce the natural enemies of these pests until temperatures are warmer, unless they are being introduced in heated greenhouses. The whitefly parasite (*Encarsia formosa*) only starts to fly, for instance, when temperatures are around 20°C. It is preferable to utilize these parasites for indoor growing, where temperatures can be regulated more easily than outdoor conditions. It is crucial to check the temperature range at which beneficial insects are active when planning for their use. Introducing insects when it is too cold, or even too hot, can lead to an expensive failure.

The length of days can also be an influencing factor on the success rate of beneficial insects. Certain natural enemies require longer days to reproduce, such as the mealybug predator (*Cryptolaemus montrouzieri*), which originates from Australia and as such is suited to climates with long sunny days and will only reproduce

in these conditions. Understanding the life cycle and temperature ranges that these insects are active at should be researched before introducing your biological pest controls.

The organization of optimum conditions for the natural enemies can be more easily managed when applying the predators in a greenhouse or conservatory. In these environments, heating can be administered to raise temperatures and windows opened when there is extreme heat. It is more difficult to influence conditions outside, but it remains vital for you to select your time of application to match the conditions in which the natural enemies will thrive. One of the most common forms of biological control used in gardens is the application of nematodes to control a wide variety of soil-borne pests, but if soil temperatures are too low, for example, the nematodes will not be active, while freezing temperatures may kill them before they have a chance to become active.

Cryptolaemus adult ladybird – a highly effective predatory beetle for the control of mealybugs. KOPPERT BIOLOGICAL SYSTEMS

Identify the Pest Correctly

Clearly establishing the identity of a pest is especially important when choosing the most effective natural enemies to control them. Identification mistakes are common. The shed white skins of aphids, for instance, are often mistaken for whitefly. This can lead to the introduction of whitefly parasites to plants, instead of the necessary aphid controls. Many parasites are host-specific and will only target certain species of insects, so introducing the wrong parasites can be expensive and delay the eventual control of the pest. There are certain natural enemies that are less specific and will feed on a wider range of insects, but it is still crucial to introduce the correct predators to the appropriate pest. Even with these generalist predators, it is sensible to time their introductions to when there is a food source.

There is plenty of valuable information and images on natural enemies and pests, with details about their life cycles, to be found online. Many books have also been printed over the years containing useful informa-tion about garden pests. These books do contain slightly less information about natural enemies, how-ever, and it is better to look online for resources about natural enemies where the information is more abun-dant. There are also techniques and tools available online that you can use in your own garden to help identify pests, such as insect-trapping products. In Chapter 3, we will look at what guides and tools can be used to aid insect identification.

Ditch the Chemicals

As a rule of thumb, synthetic and man-made chemical insecticides are bad news for beneficial insects and are largely incompatible with their use for insect pest con-trol. There have been numerous conducted studies that have looked at the short- and long-term impact of the use of insecticides on different insect groups, especially those based on neonicotinoids. This is a class of neuroactive insecticides related to nicotine that affect the nervous system. Some of the findings

Aphid skins. The skins of aphids are often left on leaves and can be mistaken for whitefly from a distance.

make for alarming reading, particularly those from a study carried out by a Spanish research group and the Entomology Department of Wageningen University (Calvo-Agudo *et al.*, 2019). This study found that some beneficial insects, such as hoverflies and aphid parasitic wasps, died within three days of feeding on honeydew produced from insects that had fed on a neonicotinoid-based insecticide applied as a soil treatment to trees. Thankfully, many of these products are no longer available and are being withdrawn from use for gardeners and growers. It is still important to check which, if any, insecticides have been used in your garden before introducing beneficial insects. Some insecticides persist on, and in, plants for long periods, with potentially long-lasting and damaging effects.

Even the more natural insecticides, such as natural pyrethrum, which is derived from chrysanthemum flowers and is permitted for use in organic growing,

can have harmful effects. Natural pyrethrum-based insecticides will break down very quickly and will not persist on plants for very long after application, but on contact with insects they are indiscriminate, killing both pests and beneficial insects. There are some more natural spray treatments that have a much-reduced impact on beneficial insects – for example, spray treatments based on less toxic substances such as seaweed and rapeseed oil are permissible. These can be used selectively when pest pressure is very high, or when conditions are not suitable for the introduction of beneficial insects.

Once you have identified which insect pests need to be confronted and have made sure that the conditions and environment are suitable for beneficial insects to survive and thrive in, the scene is set to learn more about which natural enemies to use in the garden to combat insect pests.

CHAPTER 2

THE NATURAL ENEMIES OF GARDEN PESTS

Gardeners could not be blamed for despairing over certain insect pests that descend on their gardens. These pests appear to have nothing preventing their development and nature is seemingly tilted in their favour. They do, however, have natural enemies and it is possible to use some of these enemies to turn the tide in the gardener's favour.

Nature often does have the answer, but it does not always seem to act fast enough. This is exemplified in the case of aphids, which have a reproductive capacity so fast that huge numbers can build up on plants in a matter of days, with no sign of any naturally occurring enemies to slow them down. Nature is in fact aware, as often shortly after large aphid plagues there will be a significant increase in the local ladybird population. These ladybirds are attracted to the aphids and will consume them in large numbers. This may happen more quickly if your garden is already abundant with pollen-rich plants, as advised in Chapter 1. To improve on nature's control, it is possible to supplement or introduce ladybirds and their larvae earlier into the aphid infestation. Timed introductions of ladybirds, applied as soon as aphids are observed, will slow, then control, the aphid population and limit the damage caused by their activity.

In this chapter, I will provide an overview of the different groups of insects and organisms that can be deployed to do battle with garden insect foes and will outline exactly how they work and operate.

Nematodes

One of the most versatile natural enemies for gardeners and growers is the nematode. Not all nematodes are beneficial to plants, such as the plant-parasitic nematodes, but the group used for plant protection are known as entomopathogenic nematodes (EPNs). EPNs can be used specifically to kill insect pests, while causing no harm to wildlife. These nematodes are tiny, thread-like roundworms, barely visible to the human eye. They often occur naturally in the soil and can be applied against soil-dwelling insect larvae. More recently, they are also being applied to insect larvae above ground on leaves or in the plant canopy.

There are two patterns of behaviour that the nematodes will commonly exhibit in locating their prey. These behaviours are known by the terms 'ambushing' and 'cruising'. Nematodes that showcase the ambushing behaviour will wait for their prey to

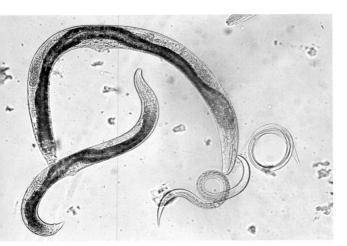

Nematodes through a microscope; these tiny eelworms are not easy to see with the human eye. D. KUCHARSKI, K. KUCHARSKA/SHUTTERSTOCK.COM

An example of nematodes delivered by a mail-order supplier.

move past them before attacking them. Nematodes that exhibit the cruising behaviour are activated to search for their prey by volatile compounds released by the target insects and then move in for the kill! This type of behaviour is most suited for nematodes seeking prey that is not very mobile, such as the vine weevil beetle larvae.

The nematodes used in horticulture and gardening are produced in huge numbers in vats not dissimilar to those used in beer production. They are then harvested and mixed with an inert natural carrier material for packing, transportation and eventual application to their target insect pest.

Instructions for Application of Nematodes

The application of nematodes is achieved by mixing the carrier and nematodes in water and then either spraying or drenching plants with the nematode solution. For above-ground applications, the nematodes are sprayed directly on to pests like caterpillars or asparagus beetle larvae on warm, damp, humid days. These conditions are vital as the nematodes require moisture to be active and survive. They are also UV-sensitive, so will die quite quickly if exposed to bright sunlight for a sustained period. For soil or compost applications, when applying nematodes against pests such as vine weevil larvae and slugs, the nematodes are watered into moist soil or compost, so that they can move and locate their targets.

Whether applied to a leaf surface or the soil, EPNs enter the pest larvae via a natural opening like a mouth or anus. Once inside, they produce a bacterium, which causes the insect to die. The body is then used as a vessel for the nematodes to reproduce in. Eventually the body decomposes and releases the new nematodes into the surrounding area. This all sounds quite gruesome for the target slug or vine weevil larva, but is a very natural form of insect pest control with no consequences for humans or wildlife. Once the nematodes run out of energy or cannot find another host, they die back to their natural levels in the soil, or die off completely in compost or on leaves.

The nematodes should be mixed in tepid water, not very cold water as this can shock them, as it would us! This would lead to poorer nematode activity and distribution. Once the nematode packs are opened, they should all be made up, as this will expose the nematodes to moisture and air, which will start to activate them. Do not leave the nematode solution

A typical way of mixing and applying nematodes with a hose-end feeder.

1. Cut open the sachet of nematodes over a bucket.

2. Mix the nematodes in a concentrate solution.

3. Stir thoroughly.

4. Transfer into a jug, ready to be poured into the hose-end feeder.

5. Pour the solution into the hose-end feeder bowl.

6. Attach the hose-end top to the feeder bowl.

7. Applying the hose-end feeder to the lawn.

8. Applying the hose-end feeder to a pot.

overnight – make sure to apply it on the day of mixing and as quickly as possible.

Equipment Required for the Application of Nematodes

The equipment required for nematode applications should also be considered. For soil or compost applications, watering cans work well if fitted with a suitable rose with a wide diameter or a coarse rose. This will prevent nematodes getting stuck in the rose and will help them to reach the target areas. Some hose-end feeders are also suitable for applying nematodes to soil or grass areas. These feeders provide a quicker method of application, which is particularly useful with larger areas such as lawns.

For leaf or above-ground applications, knapsack or small sprayers will provide a more accurate application. This is because the target pest will need to come into direct contact with the nematodes quickly, as their lifespan on the leaf is much shorter than when applied in soil or compost. When using sprayers, it is important to remove any filters, to ensure that the nematodes do not get stuck inside them. The nozzle on the sprayer should also be a coarse one, to alleviate this risk.

Storage of Nematodes

Most insect pest control nematodes will arrive in the post or by a courier. It is important to store them in a cold place or fridge if they are not being applied directly after receipt. Do not freeze them. Most suppliers will stock nematodes that can be fridge-stored for a few weeks, but not for longer. There are some nematode products that are now formulated for longer-term storage in environments like garden centres, but producer studies have shown that these formulations tend to contain less live, viable nematodes.

Different Species of Nematodes

There are several different species of EPNs produced for insect pest control. It is important to choose the right species for a particular pest. Some species will also operate at lower or higher temperatures, so it is vital to ensure that conditions are suitable for their application. The list of insect pests controlled by nematodes is extensive and increasing. At the time of writing, this list includes chafer grubs, leatherjackets, vine weevils, box tree caterpillars, slugs, asparagus beetle larvae, cutworms, fungus fly, codling moth,

An example of a hose-end feeder suitable for nematode applications – using one will speed up distribution to larger areas.

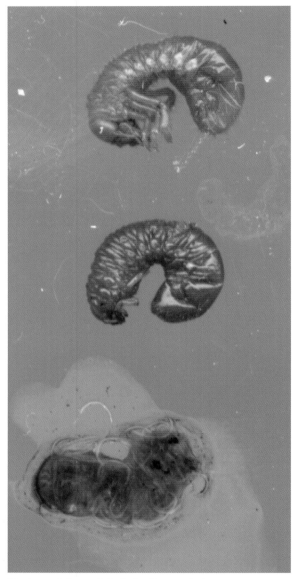

Chafer grub larvae infected with nematodes. KOPPERT BIOLOGICAL SYSTEMS.

plum fruit moth, carrot root fly and more. Further advice on applying nematodes against specific pests will follow in subsequent chapters.

Predator Natural Enemies

A more visual natural enemy is the predator. These natural enemies physically consume and eat their prey.

Many of them occur naturally and can be identified in the summer months in action on plants in gardens, feeding on various insect pests. They include ladybirds, lacewings and hoverflies.

How to Source, Store and Apply Predators

Many of these predators can now be purchased online or from mail-order companies. There are some specialist suppliers offering a wide range of beneficial insects and an increasing number of mail-order companies, such as seed companies, now listing some of the predators in their catalogues and on their websites. This is making access to the predators much easier for consumers than it used to be, and the internet provides the ideal platform for selling live products. In terms of how long predators can be stored, this can vary, but, as a general rule of thumb, one should be ready to apply the predators as quickly as possible after receiving them in the post.

Certain predators may be packed with a limited food supply so as to provide nutrition during transportation. This does get consumed quite quickly, however, and if no other food is available, some of the predators may start to eat each other! It is best to apply the predators to the plants and pests immediately upon receipt, but if this is not possible, it is good practice to store them in a cool, dark room, which will temporarily slow their activity. They can also be placed in a fridge for a short period, but the fridge should be set to a temperature that is not overly cold, otherwise the predators may be shocked and sometimes the cold can kill them. Ideally, the predators should be applied within twenty-four hours of receipt.

Application methods will depend partly on which predator is being applied and where it is in its life cycle. It is not easy to apply ladybird adults outside, for instance; they should only really be applied indoors or in contained environments. This allows a degree of management and control as to where they will feed. Even in greenhouses, however, some thought should be given as to how and when to apply winged predators, as they may fly out of open windows and doors. It is therefore good practice to close windows and doors and to leave them shut for a few hours following application. This will enable predators to acclimatize to their environments and to locate the relevant pests to feed on. Ensuring that windows or doors remain closed can of course be an issue during hot summer days, therefore in such situations it is permissible to release the predators later in the day, or in the early evening, when doors and windows can remain shut for the appropriate period of time.

Winged predators are normally supplied in bottles, plastic tubs or in cardboard sachets. One must ensure that the bottle tops are correctly removed and that containers are opened inside the area selected for application. This may sound obvious, but if the packaging is opened in one area and then moved to the application area, some predators may escape en route. Some of these products are relatively expensive, therefore it is best to be careful in terms of opening and releasing the contents, so as not to lose any valuable predators.

Once the products are situated in the appropriate application area, such as a greenhouse, the packaging should be opened as close as possible to the pest infestation. This can be achieved by, for instance, wedging the container of predators near the plant, or by tying it to the infected plant. This will ensure that the predators are released as close as possible to their prey and will begin locating and feeding on the pests as soon as possible.

If a pest infestation is widespread, one can also walk slowly up and down the greenhouse, which will allow the winged predators to fly out of their packaging. The predators will normally fly to the light, so it is advisable to cover the unopened end of the bottle, or tub, with your hands or with paper, as this will encourage the predators to exit at the remaining opened end where there is light.

The application method required for introducing the larvae of predators can be quite different to the protocol for the application of adult predators. Ladybird larvae, for instance, are very fragile and physical handling should be minimized. Containers of the larvae can be left opened next to the pests, which allows the larvae to exit of their own accord. A better method is simply to tap the container gently and brush out the larvae with a fine, small brush. This is an effective application process for both ladybird larvae and the larvae of the mealybug predatory ladybird, the *Cryptolaemus*.

Other larvae may be supplied in shaker bottles packed with a carrier material. This is the case with the lacewing larvae, which are very small and supplied in quite high numbers in a shaker bottle. The bottles, as

their name suggests, can be shaken gently and poured directly on to the infested plants. For low-growing plants, or for plants with large leaves, this is quite an easy process, but is a more difficult procedure for tall plants with narrow leaves, as the carrier material and larvae can end up being poured on to the ground. In these situations, it is better to pour the contents into small distribution boxes, which can then be hung on to the plants. The predatory larvae will then exit the boxes directly on to the plants and proceed to seek out the pests.

Ladybirds

Ladybirds are predators in both their larval and adult stages. There are over twenty-six ladybird species

Application of cryptolaemus larvae with paintbrush on to a leaf. Care should be taken when applying these fragile insects.

Distribution box. These handy small boxes can be hung on plants to help with direct distribution of various natural enemies.

present in the UK. Common species include the two-spot and seven-spot ladybirds, which provide valuable free-of-charge natural pest control in the garden. Two-spot ladybirds (*Adalia bipunctata*) are available to purchase in the UK to introduce into gardens and greenhouses, either as larvae or adults. The larvae have no wings, so can be placed directly on to plants with the aphids and will start feeding immediately. Adult ladybirds also feed on aphids, but are more difficult to introduce unless they are being used in confined spaces, such as greenhouses or conservatories.

Timing and Frequency of Application

The preferred food source for ladybird adults and larvae is that of the aphid, so it is best to apply these predators when aphids have been observed. They will sometimes feed on other insect pests, but it is better to apply them when there are aphids present. If there is no available food source, the predators may well fail to reproduce and will simply disappear. For localized treatments on specific areas of aphid activity, it is considerably easier and more efficient to choose and apply predatory larvae directly on to the infested plants. The larvae will then start feeding quickly and progress through their life cycle on, or near, the plants you wish to protect.

If a more general form of background control is desired, the adult ladybirds may be a more suitable choice of predator because they are winged. The number of applications needed to control aphid populations will depend on the severity of the infestation. Repeat applications may be required for heavier infestations, or for those that occur at a later time in the season.

Lacewings and Hoverflies

Other natural predators will only eat insect pests during one stage of their life cycle, for example lacewings and hoverflies, which eat insect pests in their larval stage. At this larval stage, they are voracious predators of aphids and other insect pests such as whitefly eggs, but as adults they will only feed on nectar and pollen. The larvae bear no resemblance to their adult form. These predators, however, are often

Seven-spot ladybird. A common species in the UK.

Two-spot ladybird (*Adalia bipunctata*), native to the UK and feeding on aphids.

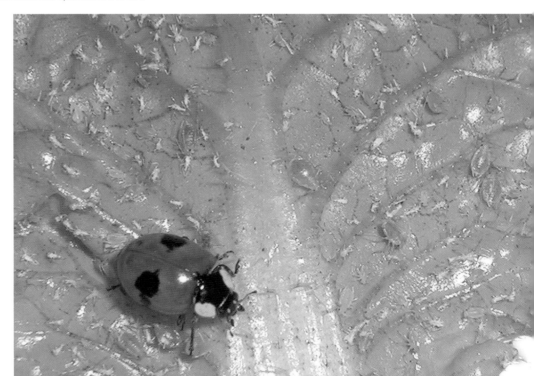

not present in the required quantity, or do not appear early enough, to rapidly control an aphid infestation. This is when we need to consider introducing predators before natural pest populations explode, but not too early and only when the pest is present. Therefore, accurate and consistent monitoring of pest levels is very important. The significance of pest monitoring is explained in Chapter 3.

If using lacewings as predators, one may find that they are normally supplied as tiny larvae inside a bottle. They should also only be used when aphids are present and applied directly on to the infested plants.

Hoverflies are also supplied by some insect producers. The hoverfly eggs are normally packaged on cards, which are then to be hung from plants. These eggs will hatch into predatory larvae that feed on the aphids. Some producers in the United States and Europe also use the same packaging formula when producing lacewing eggs on to cards, which will then also hatch into larvae and feed on aphids. The amount of predators required will again depend on the severity of the infestation.

Predatory Mites

There are more predators that can be introduced to gardens and greenhouses, including predatory mites. These tiny predators have been used in commercial greenhouse horticulture for many years. The predatory mites were used initially for control of the two-spotted spider mite (*Tetranychus urticae*), a common pest of cucumbers and tomatoes. The first predatory mite to be used in such a way is called the *Phytoseiulus persimilis*. This tiny predator cannot see, but detects spider mites by touch and scent. Plants release substances when under attack and this helps to attract the predatory mites to where the spider mites are located. They will then begin feeding on the spider mite and start reproducing themselves on the plant. This predatory mite can be used indoors and outdoors, if the climatical conditions are suitable for their use. Once the spider mite population has been consumed, the predatory-mite population stops breeding and will die off.

In recent years, more predatory mites have been discovered. These mites feed on a variety of insect pests and certain mites also feed on pollen, which enables the predatory mites to survive on plants when no pest is present. Predatory mites are normally applied using shaker bottles containing the mites and a carrier material, such as sawdust. They can also be supplied in sachets that are hung on plants, releasing the predators over several weeks. For some of the predatory mites, this represents a significant improvement in terms of how they can be deployed, as it enables their introduction before the pest is present. The sachets constantly release the predators for a number of weeks, which allows the predators to be present on the plants before the pest has actually

Lacewing larvae feeding. These tiny larvae have huge jaws for their size and are effective predators. KOPPERT BIOLOGICAL SYSTEMS

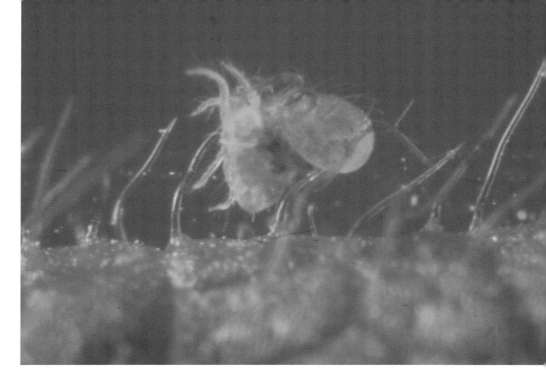

Phytoseiulus persmilis predator feeding on spider mites. The first predatory mite used on a large scale on commercially grown cucumber crops. KOPPERT BIOLOGICAL SYSTEMS

A predator release sachet releases predators for a number of weeks.

arrived, which in many cases leads to a quicker control process when it does.

Storage and Application of Predatory Mites

As is the case for other beneficial insects and natural enemies, it is better to apply the predators quickly after receipt. When applying the predators from bottles, try to keep the bottle horizontal and not vertical, as this will help to ensure that the predators are distributed throughout the bottle and not all bunched up at the top or bottom, which could lead to an uneven application. Apply the shaker bottles directly on to leaves or into distribution boxes for hanging on plants. The predators can be fridge-stored for one to two days after receipt if necessary. The predatory mites should be applied as required to combat the pest.

In terms of the predatory mites that are supplied in slow-release sachets, it is best for these to be hung on plants and, if possible, for them to be hung under a leaf or stem, so as to provide the mites a bit of shade. If some shade is provided, it will help to maintain an optimum environment inside the sachet and will prevent the sachet from drying out too quickly. If the sachet does dry out, the lifespan of the predators inside will generally be shortened as a result and fewer predators will be released.

The sachets will already be open, as they are manufactured with a small ready-made hole. The predator numbers will be building and reproduction will be occurring inside the sachet all the time, so do not worry if there are some predators located in the packaging, although this is another good reason why the sachets should be applied quickly. Most slow-release sachets will release predators for at least four weeks, so it is best to apply the predators once a month to achieve a successful preventative control programme, or to apply the sachets as soon as the first pest is observed. This process can then be repeated when required.

Applying bottles of predatory mites is an effective way to release predators more quickly and to ensure a faster establishment of predator levels. Slow-release sachets, as their name suggests, provide a slower but more measured dosage over time. The two systems can also be used in conjunction. One may wish, for example, to apply bottles of predators at the first sign of pests to establish control quickly, then opt to apply sachets afterwards, to maintain the control that was achieved going forwards.

Parasites

Some insect pests also have parasites that will attack them. If you stop to look at plants in your garden, such as roses in the summer, you will often find parasitized aphids inside. These aphids are brown in colour and mummified, often with a little hole in the back from

Predator shaker bottle application (Spidex).
KOPPERT BIOLOGICAL SYSTEMS

Aphid parasite, mummified aphid and aphid skins. A good example of an aphid parasite adult and the results of her egg-laying in the form of the mummified aphid.

which the aphid parasite has emerged. The most common genus of aphid parasites is called *Aphidius*. The life cycle of these insects reads like a scene from an *Alien* film. The tiny female parasitic wasps search out aphids and inject their own egg into the aphid. This then develops inside the aphid, killing it, before eating its way out of the aphid, to emerge as an adult parasitic wasp. These parasites are reared commercially, so can be purchased but are more suitable for release in greenhouses.

Perhaps the most well-known parasite used in bio-logical control is *Encarsia formosa*. This parasite was first observed by a tomato grower in the 1920s on his crop of tomatoes, where it was parasitizing whitefly pupae. These minute parasitic wasps have been used for many years to control whitefly populations on glasshouse-grown crops of tomatoes and cucumbers. They can also be used on other indoor-grown plants, including ornamental plants. *Encarsia formosa* are normally supplied as parasitized pupae stuck on to a card that is to be hung on plants. The tiny wasps then emerge and fly off to find whitefly larvae to parasitize. At the halfway stage of the parasite's development inside the whitefly larvae, the larvae will turn black; this provides a useful indicator of how many parasites are present in the whitefly population. If only a few of the

Encarsia formosa cards, a parasitic wasp used against whitefly. First identified by a British tomato grower.

larvae and pupae are black in colour, then more parasites are needed. Low temperatures will slow down or stop *Encarsia* development, so for most gardeners it is best to introduce them in the summer months in greenhouses.

How to Store and Apply Parasites

The natural enemies that are in the form of parasites are supplied in many shapes, sizes and stages of their life cycles. Some parasites will be supplied within their parasitized hosts, such as the *Encarsia*, where the parasites will hatch out of the already dead host insect. The parasitic wasps will then fly off to locate their prey and their next hosts. These types of products can generally be fridge-stored for one to two days, but it is better to apply them quickly. When

using *Encarsia* for whitefly control, the cards can be hung on the infected plants, or on the plants one wishes to protect from whitefly. One card can be applied per plant, as would be the application rate when applying the cards to tomatoes, for instance. All the parasites will then hatch over a period of a few days. To maintain parasite levels, some gardeners and growers will release *Encarsia* every two weeks in the summer months to maintain whitefly control.

Other parasites, including specific aphid parasites or mixes of aphid parasites, will be supplied in bottles. These bottles will sometimes contain mummified aphids from which the parasites will hatch, or the bottles may simply contain solely the adult parasites. The bottles should be opened and placed at the base of the infested plant, or tied to the plant for the parasites to exit from. As is the case with *Encarsia* applications, these parasites should be applied every two weeks during the months when there is aphid pressure, so as to help suppress aphid populations.

Most parasite-based natural enemy products are only suitable for indoor use. As with all natural enemies, it is again worth remembering that it is highly preferable to release and apply the parasites as soon as possible after receipt.

Fungi and Bacteria

Insect pests can also be attacked by natural fungi and bacteria, but few of these are available as products. The few that exist are normally licensed for use only in professional horticulture. One such natural bacteria product available to professionals is for treating caterpillar infestations, called the *Bacillus thuringiensis*. This bacterium is safe for other natural enemies and humans and provides a useful tool to use against caterpillar pests, such as cabbage whites and box tree moths. The caterpillars ingest the bacteria when feeding on leaves sprayed with it and promptly die. This product is not available to UK gardeners, unfortunately, even though it is available in some European countries. This is due to the complex and expensive licence arrangements for using such products in the UK. These rules do not apply to the introduction of beneficial insects, but there are strict rules enforcing the introduction of only native UK insects in gardens and greenhouses. The UK government will sometimes permit non-native insects to be used as natural enemies, if it can be proved that they cannot establish in the UK, or cause any harmful effects on the environment.

The success of all these forms of natural enemies depends on how, where and what they are used against, which we will now look at over the following chapters.

CHAPTER 3

TRAPPING AND IDENTIFICATION

Correctly identifying pests is the most important factor in achieving a successful pest control programme and this is especially true when using natural enemies. Many chemical pesticide treatments are broad spectrum with an impact on a variety of insect pests, so in these cases it has not always been as critical to identify correctly the precise pest. It is for such a reason that we should not be looking to use pesticides. Pesticides can be indiscriminate killers of many other insects, including beneficial ones, and can have a devastating impact on invertebrates like toads and frogs, which are also natural predators of insect pests like slugs. Natural enemies of insect pests tend to be selective with their targets and some are very precise, especially if they are a parasite.

Having some insight, knowledge and recognition of the insect pest species is important for a successful biological control programme. Misidentification can be commonplace and another example of this is when aphids and leaf hoppers are confused. The appearance of leaf hoppers and their shredded skins can often be confused with that of aphids, which can result in the incorrect application of natural predators. Attempting to apply the correct natural enemy, when aphids are present, can also be complex, as

certain aphid parasites will not parasitize every species of aphid. Some predators of insect pests can be a little less selective, such as lacewing larvae and ladybirds, which will feast on most species of aphids and other soft-bodied insect pests like spider mite. This is more of a side effect, however, than a predator specifically eating such multiple pests. It therefore remains important to select the best predator for the present insect pest.

Aids to Identification

The internet is a valuable tool for seeking out information and images and most search engines will lead you to the right place, although not always! The Royal Horticultural Society website contains a useful guide that is a good starting point for garden pest identification. The RHS also provides a list of biological control suppliers and explains which insects they sell. An additional reference source from the RHS is the book *Pests & Diseases*, by Pippa Greenwood and Andrew Halstead. This publication provides useful descriptions of diseases and pests, along with plentiful illustrations. The book was first published in 1997, so there is not too much information on the latest biological controls available, but the book is handy for early diagnosis of pests.

Specific websites and books on the natural enemies of insect pests are slightly more difficult to source for the hobby or amateur grower or gardener. There are professional publications, which can still serve as valuable resource guides, especially for information on insect life cycles and pictorial guides to the natural enemies in action. An excellent example of such is the publication from Koppert Biological Systems entitled *Knowing and Recognizing: The Biology of Glasshouse Pests and their Natural Enemies,* by M.H. Malais and W.J. Ravensberg.

There is one small, very important investment that should be considered when beginning to use biological control and natural enemies – a small magnifying glass. This will help you to identify the relevant pests and how many natural enemies are present, and whether you will need to introduce more. The linen tester magnifying glass types, such as the one pictured here, are of strong magnification and help to keep the lens the correct distance from the leaf, so that you may easily identify the insects.

One of the most useful tools for monitoring insect pests is insect traps. These are available in several different formats and it is important to know when, where and how to use each type of trap.

Sticky Traps

These traps are very common and are designed for use indoors, in structures such as greenhouses, polythene tunnels or even conservatories. They are too indiscriminate to use outdoors, as they mainly use colour as the mechanism to attract and catch flying insects. They are often coloured yellow, which will attract many insects. You may have already noticed first-hand the attractiveness of yellow colouring to insects if you wear yellow clothing, or drive a yellow car, for instance. The traps are coated with glue, which holds the inset to the trap once it has been attracted to it. The sticky traps provide an excellent early warning to the presence of certain insect pests, including whitefly, winged aphids, sciarid fly and thrips. Some of these pests can remain undetected on plants if sticky traps are not used to monitor them. The early detection of these pests can help prevent large populations from establishing.

It is also worth drawing your attention to the wide variety of sticky traps available. Some of these traps are better suited for monitoring purposes and others for the mass trapping of flying insect pests. Sticky traps with release papers can be used as reasonably efficient monitoring traps. This is because one side, or segment, of paper from the trap can be removed to expose the sticky glue. This enables you to count the insects caught on the exposed glue after a few days, or a week. The other side is then exposed the following week by removing the release paper, then counting and comparing the insects caught to the previous weeks' catch. If there are more insects, this can be an indication that the pest levels are rising. This exercise can be repeated weekly to provide a guide as to whether pest levels are rising or falling.

More traditional sticky traps have no release papers and are normally supplied stuck together, requiring you to peel the traps from each other before hanging them out. These traps provide an extremely sticky surface area in which to catch flying insect pests in mass numbers. This assists in not only informing you which pests are present, but also in physically reducing the numbers of such pests. If using the traps in such a way, it is important to replenish them frequently, as they can

Linen tester magnifying glass.

A cardboard version of a sticky trap is more eco-friendly than the plastic alternatives.

quickly fill up with insects, dust and debris. It is easy to forget this, which leads to a non-functioning trap suspended in the greenhouse catching nothing.

As a general guide for placement, sticky traps should be situated just above the growing heads of plants. When plants are small, the sticky traps can be fixed to the small canes and inserted into the pots. When the plants or crop are growing, the sticky traps should then be hung above the growing tips and raised higher as the plants grow. The success of this strategy can be evidenced in the case of tomatoes, for instance, as adult whitefly like to congregate in the heads of the plants and once disturbed will fly up and be easily caught on the yellow sticky trap.

There are also different colours of sticky traps, with yellow being the most common and frequently used as it is a general attractor. Another option, however, is the blue sticky trap. This trap was designed primarily to attract tiny thrip adults without catching lots of other insects, although other insects do unfortunately get caught on them, including parasitic wasps and occasionally bumblebees. It is apparent therefore that, for general greenhouse use, yellow traps remain the most advantageous. There can also be some limited use of different coloured traps outside, including orange traps for attracting carrot root fly.

Pheromone Traps

These traps are used to monitor moth populations and provide an important tool to the gardener for indicating advance warning of impending caterpillar attack. These traps are supplied with pheromone lures that are very specific to individual moth species. The lures contain a sex pheromone that attracts the male moths. The male moths detect the scent and mistake it for female moths. They will proceed to follow the scent of the pheromone lure directly to the trap, where they are then captured. This prevents them from mating and indirectly reduces female egg laying. Pheromone traps alone do not control moth populations, however. They are primarily monitoring traps that should be utilized to inform you when moths are active. This can often help with the timing of natural pest controls for the caterpillar stage of the life cycle.

There are various designs of pheromone traps. There are the Deltatraps, for instance, which look like an open-ended tent. These traps are suspended from trees or bushes and moths will fly into them, getting caught on the sticky glue inside. Other insects and even small birds, unfortunately, may also fly in by accident. To avoid such scenarios, there are plastic funnel-like traps available, which will funnel the moths into a small bucket. These traps do not generally use glue and are more likely only to capture the target moths. Some of these traps enable a small amount of water to be placed in the bottom of the funnel bucket, or alternatively a piece of sticky trap can be applied, to ensure that the moths cannot escape. If large populations of moths are present and an understanding is required as to whether the population is rising or falling, count the number of moths caught weekly then remove them, so that you may compare this with the next weeks' catch. Plastic funnel pheromone traps can also be reused for many years, if the pheromone lures are replaced in the moth flying season. It is also good practice to put the traps away in a store or shed when not in use, as this will help to maintain the trap in good condition. If the traps are left in constant exposure to the sun, they may go brittle and eventually break.

There are also several different formats for the pheromone lures supplied with pheromone traps. The original and most common type of lures are supplied as small rubber bungs, which are infused with the

A castellation design is a more targeted version of a pheromone trap, as its design prevents capture of other insects.

Horse-chestnut leaf miner trap and pheromone lures. An example of a pheromone trap used for catching horse-chestnut leaf miner moths.

pheromone. The pheromone is not visible and is normally released for a period of roughly six weeks. There are also pheromone lures supplied in clear plastic vials. These release the pheromone lure through the plastic and are claimed to provide a more even release over a set period. Some companies have also developed 'long-life' lures and claim that these lures release the pheromone over the entire moth flying season.

Pheromone traps should be placed, or hung, on the trees, shrubs or plants where the moths are expected. Resist the temptation to set up too many pheromone traps in one area, as this can be self-defeating by rendering ineffective the attractant of the lures. Follow the supplier guidelines as to how many pheromone traps are required for a specifically sized area or number of trees. Most pheromone traps and lures will provide coverage of larger areas than you would expect.

There are some key factors to remember when using pheromone traps:

- Ensure that you have the correct pheromone lure for the specific moth species.
- Place the trap and lure when moths are flying. In the UK, this is from May onwards for most moths, though not for all species.
- Replace the pheromone lure according to the frequency recommended by the manufacturer. Most lures have an active life of about six weeks, but there are 'long-life' versions.
- Keep unopened or disused pheromone lures in a freezer for long-term storage, or in a fridge for short-term storage.

Mating disruptors are also available in some countries. These confuse the male moths so that they are unable to locate female moths. This is used as a form of biological control of moths, but is not yet permitted for use in the UK by hobby gardeners. It is, however, being tested by professional users in large gardens and estates.

Attractant Traps

These traps are often similar in design to pheromone funnel traps, but do not contain a pheromone sex lure; instead, they contain an attraction lure. This lure can be floral, for example, so that it gives off a scent that will attract the target insect. There are a variety of ways in which these attractants are supplied. Some are

A chafer beetle trap that uses a floral scent to attract and catch adult chafer beetles.

supplied as liquids in vials and others are infused into sticky pads. These attractants are used in several flying beetle traps, such as the garden chafer traps and raspberry beetle traps.

The timing of when to apply these traps is even more critical than with the other pheromone traps, however, as often the beetles are not flying for long periods. It is thus important to understand the life cycle of the beetle that you are trying to catch. This is especially true for garden chafer beetles (more detail provided in Chapter 8). There is also research underway attempting to discover a suitable attractant for vine weevil beetles. Attractant lures tend to have a shorter lifespan than pheromone lures, so I must reiterate that careful timing is required with their use. Unopened lures can also be fridge stored.

Pitfall Traps

These are my least favourite type of trap, as many of their designs often lead to beneficial insects, such as rove beetles, falling into them. Pitfall traps are placed in the soil and allow insects to drop into them. The attractiveness of the trap is increased to slugs and snails when beer is added. Personally, I would rather keep the beer for drinking and control slugs with other biological methods, such as the use of nematodes.

A typical pitfall trap used to catch slugs and snails, often baited with beer. OBEKI.COM

Once we have identified the pests we need to control and formulated an understanding of how serious potential pest infestations might be, we can start to piece together a plan for controlling and preventing the damage they may cause. The following chapters will provide a guide as to the options available for different plant groups and the most common types of pests that might attack them.

CHAPTER 4

PROTECT FROM THE START

A clean start to your growing season is very important for future battles against insect pests, especially at the propagation stage. Young plants are vulnerable to attack from pests and diseases due to their less developed root systems and limited top growth, making the potential attack of insect pests more serious than it would be to older, more robust plants. Helping plants to develop a strong root system quickly will enable them to grow strongly and develop the ability to survive early pest and disease attacks. The addition of biostimulants at the propagation stage will aid this process (see Chapter 10).

If you are purchasing more mature plants, especially in large pots, it is worth checking with the nursery if they have been treated for vine weevil control. It is very easy to unknowingly introduce vine weevil into your garden if the larvae are already present in the pots. A visible indicator of vine weevil activity is clear if you observe 'half-moon' cut marks on the leaves, created by the feeding adult vine weevils. It can also be useful to know if the nursery producer is using chemical pest control or biological pest control. If it is chemical, there may be some remaining chemical residues on plants that could slow or impair the use of natural enemies on those plants at a later stage.

Good Hygiene

The first step, even before propagation, is ensuring that growing areas are clean, with good hygiene and weed-free areas and surfaces. Insect pests are very adept at hiding in cracks and crevices or overwintering on weeds and leaf litter. Whitefly and aphids are often found on weeds in empty glasshouses, even in the winter, or under benches where weeds or stock plants have been left. These pests are quite capable of surviving low temperatures and in a mild winter they will easily survive in an unheated greenhouse. Such a location is ideal for their survival before they transfer to the fresh new plants. Other pests, such as spider mites, will migrate to greenhouse roof structures and remain there over the winter, barely alive, but just retaining enough energy to make it through the winter. As day lengths extend and temperatures rise in the spring, the spider mites will move on to newly growing plants and start to feed again. In areas such as conservatories, mealybugs will find holes in the walls to hide in, or in the bark or plant stems of more mature plants. Once they are situated in such places, it can be difficult to dislodge them. It is best to control the population levels of spider mites and mealybugs while they are on

Typical damage from adult vine weevil showing on a leaf as 'half-moon' cut marks. D. KUCHARSKI, K. KUCHARSKA/
SHUTTERSTOCK.COM

plants, before winter arrives, and therefore avoid the potential for annual infestations.

Cleaning and washing pots is also important as it is easy for pests, like root mealybug, to hide in old pots and quickly attack the roots of new plants freshly planted into such pots. These pests can also hide under floor matting, so where possible clean and disinfect the under-matting of floors and plant benches. There are some good disinfectant products available to be added to water, which can improve the cleaning process, but check the label to ensure that they are suitable for use as pot and floor cleaners, and make sure to wear protective clothing such as rubber gloves when using them.

Another method that can be implemented to help clean greenhouses is through the use of fumigator smokes. These fumigators used to contain quite lethal insecticides, but thankfully most of these are no longer permitted for use in horticulture or gardening, and they have been replaced with more natural products. These new fumigator products do have some real benefits. Some contain garlic, for instance, which aids the natural resistance of plants to pests and diseases. These fumigators also act as a natural dispersant of insect pests. This makes them an ideal tool for cleansing greenhouses.

Ensure to take care when using these fumigators. Close all vents and windows before placing the fumer on a flat surface on the ground. Proceed to light the fumer and vacate the greenhouse quickly. It is preferable to leave the greenhouse shut and not to enter it for several hours; if possible, leave it overnight. If using a garlic-based fumigator there is no need to remove plants, but if using certain sulphur fumers you may need to, so ensure to read the relevant instructions and labels carefully. The fumers can be used at the end of the season as a clean-up process, or prior to the start of the season to ensure a clean beginning. The smoke can even be used at propagation if no natural enemies are being introduced at that time.

Pest Control at Propagation

Even your choice of compost can influence the amount of insect pests that will find their way to your new plants. One of the most common pests at propagation is loosely known as the fungus fly or fungus gnat. This actually describes several fly species, including sciarid flies and shore flies, but it is the sciarid fly (*Bradysia paupera*) that normally appears and reaches

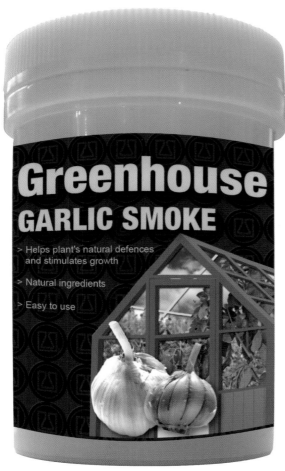

An example of a natural fumigator for greenhouses that uses garlic.

Plants being propagated at London's oldest garden, Chelsea Physic Garden – a garden that now uses biological pest control.

Sciarid Flies

Adult sciarid flies can arrive in very high numbers and tend to fly upwards when plants are disturbed. At this stage in their life cycle they are a nuisance, but they are not damaging the plants. This cannot be said of their larval stage, however. The eggs that are laid in the compost quickly develop into tiny white larvae with a black head. They will feed on plant roots and can spread plant diseases, such as pythium, which can cause plant death especially in cuttings and young plants. The sciarid larvae prefer to feed on rotting dead plants, but will feed on live young plant roots and can spread viruses and harmful fungi. The warmer the temperature, the quicker the life cycle of the sciarid flies. Propagation benches are often heated, and young plants and seedlings are often grown in warm propagation boxes, which will only accelerate the life cycle of the flies. At 20°C plus, the life cycle of the flies, from egg to adult, will take about three weeks, with adult flies living for about a week.

To monitor and control the adult sciarid flies, place yellow sticky traps just above the young plants. Once the plants are disturbed, the traps will catch high numbers of sciarid flies. Shore flies often sit on a bench

the highest numbers. This group of flies like to lay their eggs in organic matter, so a peat-based compost, or an alternative containing plentiful organic matter, will attract the flies. They thrive in the humid, warm conditions that are often met when growing young plants. Overwatering the plants at this stage also increases the damp, warm environment that this pest thrives in, and the formation of algae on the compost surface further enhances this. Shore flies will lay most of their eggs in other areas such as damp, wet patches on soil floors. This is where good hygiene pays off, as by keeping areas under benches clean and free of damp, there is less chance of creating standing-water areas prone to growing algae.

Sciarid fly larvae. The larval stage of sciarid is the most damaging part of its life cycle to plants. KOPPERT BIOLOGICAL SYSTEMS

Sciarid fly adult. These flies can appear in high numbers and fly upwards when disturbed. D. KUCHARSKI, K. KUCHARSKA/
SHUTTERSTOCK.COM

surface, so it is best to place a sticky trap horizontally on the bench surface with only the upper glue side exposed, which will catch more of the shore fly adults. If fly numbers are high, increase the number of yellow traps.

Trapping alone will not control the fungus fly populations, however, and the application of natural enemies in the form of entomopathogenic nematodes (*see* Chapter 2) is recommended. These tiny eelworm-like organisms are effective against many different insect pests and sciarid fly larvae control is a prime example of where the nematodes provide a highly effective biological control. Nematodes are watered into the compost, or growing media, that you are using to propagate plants. This might be a tray of cuttings, plug plants or freshly transplanted young plants. Normally this is carried out once sciarid fly adults have been identified or caught on traps.

Once the nematodes have been applied, they will move through the compost searching for the pest larvae that are normally located at or around the plant roots. The nematodes then enter the larvae, releasing a natural bacterium that will kill them. Due to the tiny size of the larvae and where they are situated, it is difficult to observe the dead larvae, but fly numbers will start to decline a few days after the first nematode application. This can be noted by the fly counts on sticky traps, or just by a general observation that fly levels are lower, with less flying around when the plants are disturbed.

Several nematode species can be used for sciarid fly control, but the most effective species are called the *Steinernema feltiae*. If there are very high numbers of sciarid fly, a repeat application may be required. Nematodes can be applied as a preventative application, but will run out of energy if no sciarid fly larvae are found within a few weeks of application.

Another option for the control of sciarid fly is the introduction of tiny soil-dwelling predatory mites. These predators are scavengers that feed on sciarid fly larvae, thrip pupae and other small pest larvae that they locate on top of, or just under, the soil surface. There are two common species of predators produced and applied for this purpose: *Hypoaspis miles* (now renamed, but not commonly known as *Stratiolaelaps scimitus*); and the *Macrocheles robustulus*. These predators are normally supplied in tubes or bottles mixed with a carrier material, such as vermiculite, or, in the case of *Macrocheles*, some compost. The bottle contents should be applied directly to the compost or soil surface, but not directly on the plants. This helps to ensure that the predators can quickly scurry away to locate pest larvae. The predators can survive for quite long periods, so generally only need applying once during the propagation of plants.

Macrocheles robustulus. A soil-borne predatory mite with a big appetite for small larvae that it finds in compost, like sciarid fly larvae.
KOPPERT BIOLOGICAL SYSTEMS

Professional propagation nurseries will release these predators into the area where they are propagating. This is either directly on to seed trays or pots with young plants, and sometimes under benches, so that these predators will feed on any pest larvae that are on the soil beneath the propagating benches. They can provide a useful background control for nuisance flies like the sciarid and shore fly, and other glasshouse pests like thrips. There is also a small rove beetle that can be introduced called the *Atheta coriaria*. These are sometimes released in a breeding bucket to feed on fly larvae, but they can be difficult to establish and are not generally available in the smaller units that hobby growers and gardeners can use.

Slugs

A tray of seedlings, or a row of newly potted plants, may also capture the attention of other pests looking for a food source, especially as they emerge from their winter slumber or hibernation. Watch out for slime trails on bench surfaces, which will indicate the presence of snails or slugs. Slugs will find a greenhouse a very suitable place to overwinter. When such a greenhouse is presented with newly germinated seedlings, or fresh young plants, it will provide them with an ideal food source. They will very quickly damage and destroy young plants if they are left untreated.

Sometimes the presence of slugs will be harder to notice, as much of their feeding is done at night. Covering trays and pots at night will help to protect young plants, but this is not always practical. An easy way to deter these nocturnal pests is with the use of non-poisonous slug pellets, such as those that contain ferric phosphate. These pellets can be sprinkled under benches and on the compost surface of pots and trays to protect young plants. I will explain the use of these pellets further in Chapter 6.

Aphids and Whiteflies

In the summer months, aphids and whitefly may also locate the new plants, and I will explain how to control them in the next chapter on greenhouse pests, but at the propagation stage, the most useful tool to monitor and control their presence is with the use of yellow sticky traps (*see* previous chapter).

Leafhoppers

Leafhoppers can also leave their mark on new plants. These aphid-sized insects are sapsuckers and will leave patches of silvery damage on leaves. They also

Safe slug pellets. Not all slug pellets use harmful poisons.

Leafhoppers are often mistaken for aphids and will leave white marks on leaves where they feed. MUDDY KNEES/ SHUTTERSTOCK.COM

Springtails. These insects feed on organic matter and are largely harmless unless occurring in large numbers. HOLGER KIRK/SHUTTERSTOCK.COM

often shed their skins on the plants, as aphids do. The adults are winged and will fly off when disturbed, so some can therefore be caught on sticky traps. The damage they cause, however, tends to be largely cosmetic and will occur primarily on plants such as mint, so they are not considered a serious pest deserving of too much concern.

Springtails

Springtails can also damage young roots and seedlings. They are not generally a serious pest, however, and most plants, when they grow out of the seedling stage, are not vulnerable to attack from these small wingless insects. Some soil-borne predatory mites, such as *Hypoaspis*, will also feed on them.

Mice

Greenhouses can also offer a winter home for larger pests like mice, which may opt to nest in packets of seeds. Although they are not often considered a plant pest, they can consume the tops of plants, leaving them with just their roots. This book, however, does not cover natural enemies of small animals! If you therefore suspect their presence, an old-fashioned mouse trap or two should provide the solution.

Once plants have established root systems and healthy top growth, many of the pests at the propagation stage are no longer a threat to them. Protecting the plants at this stage is therefore very important for a future of successful development. The plants' increased development and flowering does, however, attract another set of insect pests, which we will now look at in the next chapter.

CHAPTER 5

GREENHOUSE PESTS AND THEIR NATURAL ENEMIES

Greenhouses are an ideal environment for insect pests, as they provide a warm environment in which insects can feed and reproduce in high numbers. Often greenhouses are full of young tender plants, fruiting plants such as tomatoes, or pollen-rich ornamental plants, all of which provide insect pests with the food they are looking for. The good news is that these same conditions are ideal for establishing the natural enemies of such pests. Greenhouses also provide a confined environment where it is possible to manage and develop natural enemy populations. They provide an optimum environment for biological control that can be more difficult to establish in outdoor situations. There are many different pests that can establish in greenhouses, but I will focus on the more commonly occurring pests and explain how to control them naturally.

Aphids

Aphids are one of the fastest growing pests in terms of their reproductive capacity, not even needing to mate, and in many cases producing live young aphids without going through the process of egg laying, before they are found on plants indoors. The name aphid can refer to several different species, including blackfly and greenfly. Aphid species that occur commonly in greenhouses include the melon cotton aphid (*Aphis gossypii*), glasshouse potato aphid (*Aulacorthum solani*), green-peach aphid (*Myzus persicae*) and the potato aphid (*Macrosiphum euphorbiae*).

Aphids are sapsuckers, extracting the plant sap to gain nutrients and proteins. The sap is high in sugars, which are then excreted back on to the plants in the form of honeydew. This often makes plants sticky and the excrement will grow black mould. Aphid feeding will stunt plant growth and reduce photosynthesis in leaves. Growing points can also develop in a distorted way as aphids transmit plant viruses, which can cause fruit to distort and leaves to curl up. Certain species of aphids will overwinter on host plants and then move on to other plants in the spring, while others do not. The aphids that do overwinter on host plants tend to migrate to woody plants in the autumn and lay eggs that overwinter. For a large portion of the life cycle of most aphids, they are asexual and produce live young. This can result in very large numbers appearing on

Kerley & Co. greenhouse. A view inside one of the UK's leading plant breeders. They also utilize biological control against insect pests.

Aphids (*Aphis gossypii*). A common species of aphid found in the UK.
KOPPERT BIOLOGICAL SYSTEMS

plants in a relatively short period of time and explains why this pest can be so destructive to so many different plant types.

Aphid Natural Enemies

Fortunately, there are many aphid predators and parasites in nature. Outdoors, many small bird species will feast on aphids. Wasps, during their nest-building stage, will also harvest aphids to feed their young. In the insect world, there are also plenty of natural enemies that will feed on aphids. Some of these can also be purchased from biological control producers to supplement the control provided by nature, especially in greenhouses.

Aphid Parasites

If the doors and vents of greenhouses are open, you may attract some of these natural enemies inside, but generally this will be too late due to the rapid reproductive rate of aphids. It is sensible to be ahead of the aphid population growth, if possible. One of the best ways of achieving this is with the use of aphid parasites. These are available as tiny parasitic wasps, which are very effective at searching for aphids, especially individual aphids or small colonies. Once a parasitic wasp has located an aphid, it will touch it with its antennae. This is firstly so that the wasp can understand if this is a species it will parasitize and secondly to enable it to clarify if the aphid has already been parasitized. Once identified, the parasite will inject its egg into the aphid. This parasitic wasp will then develop inside the aphid, eventually killing it and hatching out to pursue more aphids.

It can be quite difficult first identifying which type of aphid species your plants are infested with and also knowing which parasite should then be introduced. To solve this potential confusion, it is possible to purchase aphid parasite mixes. These contain several different parasites, enough to account for all the common major species in the UK. This combination of parasites can be introduced when the first aphids are expected or observed. It is easy to release the parasites – simply

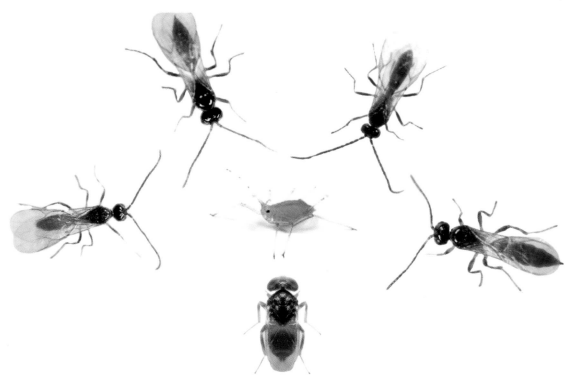

Aphiscout is a product that uses a clever combination of different aphid parasite species to control aphids. KOPPERT BIOLOGICAL SYSTEMS

open their container in the greenhouse and utilize the handy sticky label that some versions come supplied with, which can be used as a hanger for the product when strapped to the plant.

Aphid Predators

There are circumstances in which aphid parasites alone cannot control a large aphid population. This can occur when a large aphid population quickly arrives on plants. The aphid parasites do not like getting covered in the sticky honeydew that the aphids produce, so may leave large colonies alone and target individual or smaller colonies. To overcome this problem, we must look to aphid predators that have no such misgivings about attacking large colonies.

Some of these predators, such as hoverflies and ladybirds, may appear naturally in greenhouses if windows or doors are left open. Waiting for these predators to arrive, however, can be a risky policy and it is better to introduce aphid predators as soon as large colonies are observed. There are several aphid predators, such as ladybirds and lacewings, available to purchase from biological control suppliers. So, which predator to choose?

For low-growing plants, such as lettuce, or plants with large leaf surfaces, choose the lacewing larvae. These voracious, tiny larvae have a big appetite and are capable of consuming large numbers of aphids. The lacewing larvae are normally supplied in a bottle with a carrier material and should be sprinkled over the aphid-infested plants. The lacewing larvae are largely nocturnal, so can be difficult to observe in the day, but at night they will feast on many aphids. The larvae have quite a long life cycle and will develop into adult lacewings after roughly six weeks. The adults do not feed on aphids and will disperse quite quickly. Repeat applications can be made where and when aphid populations establish. Lacewings require a minimum temperature of about 15°C to be active.

For larger plants, such as aubergines or large ornamental plants, ladybird larvae can be applied directly

Lacewing adult (*Chrysoperla carnea*). This stage of the lacewing life cycle does not feed on insects. HENRI KOSKINEN/
SHUTTERSTOCK.COM

to infested plants. If applying adult ladybirds, however, be careful to release them with doors and windows shut to prevent them flying out. The adults are more mobile than the larvae and if they do not locate food quickly, they may attempt to exit the greenhouse. Ladybird larvae can be fragile and do not always transport well in the post, so careful handling is required upon receipt and it is important to release them as soon as you can.

Another aphid predator available from some biological control suppliers is the *Aphidoletes* gall midge. These gall midges are supplied as pupae, which hatch into gall midges that will then go on to detect aphid colonies. They will lay eggs in, or near the aphid colonies, and these eggs will develop into small, orange-coloured larvae that suck out the contents of the aphids' bodies!

The key to success with aphid control is introducing natural enemies early and reacting quickly if you notice aphid colonies developing. A greenhouse provides the ideal environment for aphids to breed quickly, but does so also for their natural enemies, which can thrive in a confined space like a greenhouse, conservatory or polythene tunnel.

Red Spider Mites

A pest with a rather misleading name, as for most of its active life it is green with two black spots and known as the two-spotted spider mite (*Tetranychus urticae*). This small mite can reproduce rapidly in warm temperatures and, despite it not being winged, can spread over quite large areas. The mites may travel leaf to leaf, or move

Gall midge larva – the larval stage of a gall midge, which is an effective aphid control. KOPPERT BIOLOGICAL SYSTEMS

Two-spotted spider mite. A common pest in glasshouses and on strawberries. TOMASZ KLEJDYSZ/SHUTTERSTOCK.COM

Red spider mite leaf damage on a cucumber plant. A.J. CESPEDES/SHUTTERSTOCK.COM

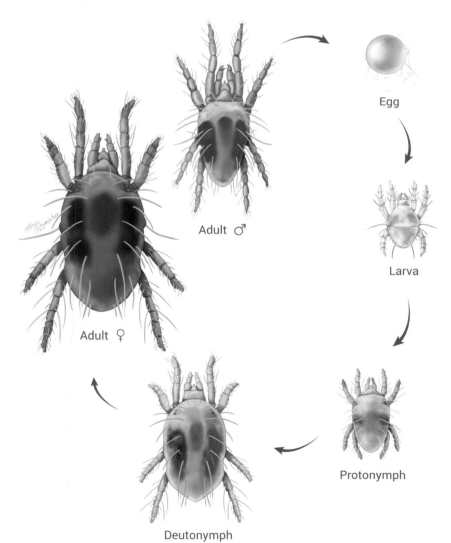

Egg

Larva

Adult ♂

Adult ♀

Protonymph

Deutonymph

Spider mite life cycle – how a two-spotted spider mite develops. KOPPERT BIOLOGICAL SYSTEMS

Phytoseiulus persimilis predator eating spider mite. A natural enemy devouring its prey. KOPPERT BIOLOGICAL SYSTEMS

on the tiny web-like threads that it can produce; webs that are also moved by air currents, or even on the clothing of gardeners working or walking near the plants. The mite damages plants by sucking out leaf contents and can inject harmful substances into plants. This makes the leaves go yellow and if the mites are high in numbers a whole plant may die. Spider mites often target and attack tomatoes, cucumbers and ornamental plants in greenhouses.

The young and adult stages of the spider mite life cycle will feed on leaves. As days start to shorten, the spider mites are triggered into a kind of hibernation known as diapause. The mites will then stop feeding and seek to find a suitable location to overwinter, which is often in the greenhouse roof or structure. The mites will start to turn red when they are going into diapause and are very difficult to kill once they are at this stage of their development, as they are barely alive and are difficult for the predators to feed on.

Spider Mite Predators

The control of spider mites in greenhouses using predatory mites was one of the first biological controls employed on a commercial scale in glasshouses and has been used by professional growers for many years. It has proven to be a far more effective form of control than that of insecticides, as spider mites are clever at building resistance to these, which has rendered them largely useless and led to a big reduction in their use. This is good for both the environment and plants, which grow more healthily without the application of insecticides.

Phytoseiulus Persimilis

The most effective and commonly used spider predator is called *Phytoseiulus persimilis*. This predatory mite likes warm conditions and at 20°C the female will lay eggs faster than spider mites. The predators eat all stages of the spider mite life cycle and are red in colour. The predators are also about twice the size of the spider mites and can move relatively quickly across the plant.

A recent development has been the rearing and release of pale-coloured *Phytoseiulus persimilis* that change colour once they have fed on spider mites, which is rather neat and provides clear proof of predation. *Phytoseiulus persimilis* are supplied in shaker bottles containing a carrier material. These mites are applied by shaking out the bottle contents over the leaves of plants infested with spider mites. The predators then disperse to consume the spider mite and begin breeding on the plant. How quick this control will be established depends on the spider mite population. If there are high numbers of spider mites in webbing, quite a high number of predators may be required and it may take more than one application and several weeks to control. Once the spider mite is controlled, the predators will die and will need reintroducing if spider mite reappear.

Amblyseius Californicus

Another predatory mite that can be used in greenhouses, introduced before spider mite appear and that will continue to breed after they have been controlled, is the *Amblyseius californicus*. This predatory mite will control smaller spider mite populations and feed on pollen to supplement its diet.

Amblyseius californicus can also be supplied in slow-release sachets. These sachets are hung on plants, releasing predators for about four weeks. They should be introduced when spider mite are expected, then reintroduced about every four weeks. This maintains a constant number of predators on plants to patrol and pick off spider mites. These predators do not like going into the red spider mite webs, so if webbing is present *Phytoseiulus persimilis* should be the first-choice predator. The two predators, in the optimum conditions, can be applied in combination.

Amblyseius californicus predatory mite. This predator can also feed on pollen, thus extending its time on plants and providing extended control of spider mites.
KOPPERT BIOLOGICAL SYSTEMS

A Note on Temperature

The control of spider mites using predatory mites can be very effective in greenhouses, as long as the temperature is 15°C plus. However, *Phytoseiulus* does not thrive in very hot, dry conditions with low humidity, so in this type of environment the other choice of predator, *Amblyseius californicus*, may function more effectively. A handy tip to help *Phytoseiulus persimilis* predators remain active and stay at the top of plants in hot weather is to mist the tops of plants when temperatures are high. This increases the local humidity on the plant and disrupts the spider mites, which prefer hot, dry conditions.

Whiteflies

Whiteflies, like aphids, are another sapsucking insect and a common pest found in greenhouses. These small flies have white wings and normally congregate on the underside of leaves. Once the leaves are disturbed, they will often fly up. Eggs are laid on leaves that develop into flat larvae, which feed on the leaves as the adults do. As the larvae feed, they also excrete sticky sugars, referred to as honeydew, on to plants. This will often grow black mould on it, making plants quite unsightly. The whiteflies will weaken plants with their feeding, stunting growth and causing leaves to fall off.

Whitefly Natural Enemies

Encarsia Formosa

For many years, the tiny parasitic wasp, *Encarsia formosa*, has been introduced into greenhouses for the biological control of whiteflies and remains the most effective natural enemy against this pest. In recent years, however, some predatory mites have also been found to feed on whitefly eggs and can therefore be introduced to plants in greenhouses to assist in the control of whitefly.

Most of the adult *Encarsia* are female and search for whitefly larvae in which to lay their eggs. As the *Encarsia* develop, they turn the whitefly pupae black, which can be observed on the underside of leaves. This results in the death of the whitefly and the emergence of a new

Whitefly life cycle – how
a whitefly develops
from egg to adult.
KOPPERT BIOLOGICAL
SYSTEMS

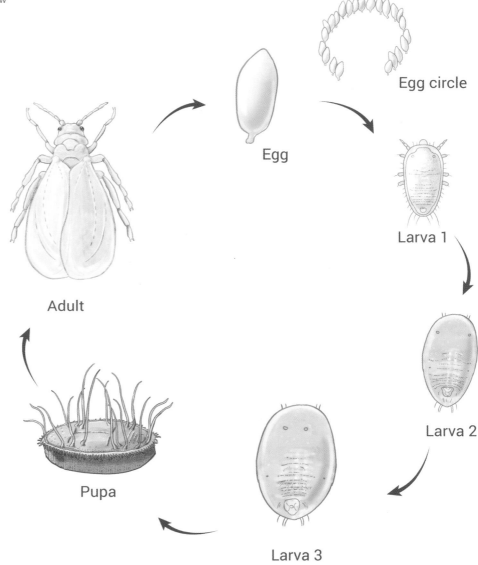

Egg circle

Egg

Larva 1

Larva 2

Adult

Larva 3

Pupa

Encarsia adult, which will then fly off to seek out more whitefly to attack. *Encarsia* activity is influenced by temperature and they are most active at 20°C plus. They can remain active at lower temperatures, but may not be able to keep up with the whitefly populations.

Encarsia are normally supplied as parasitized black pupae stuck on to cards. These cards are then hung on plants and the adult wasps will emerge from the pupae within a few days. It is possible that some adults may have already emerged in the packaging when delivered by mail order, so ensure that packages are opened carefully within the greenhouse where they are being applied and not in the kitchen! The most effective way to use these parasites is in the form of regular introductions. This maintains their presence to protect plants at vulnerable times and helps to build up *Encarsia* numbers.

For hobby growers, application may be desirable as soon as adult whitefly are observed on plants, or on yellow sticky traps. If using sticky traps, do not have too many up at once, as the adult *Encarsia* may get caught on them, and do not hang the cards near the traps. It takes time for the whitefly pupae to go black, so although the *Encarsia* will be actively looking for whitefly as soon as they are released, it might be several weeks before black pupae are observed on the underside of leaves. If the percentage of black parasitized pupae is low, the number of cards may need to be increased, as the parasites might not be keeping up with the whitefly population. This is more likely when temperatures are lower, which slows down *Encarsia* activity.

Predatory Mites

In recent years, some beneficial insect producers have also been advising the introduction of some of their predatory mites normally used for red spider mite or thrip control, for control of the egg stage of the whitefly life cycle. Some of these predators have the advantage of being active at lower temperatures than the *Encarsia*. One such predator is the *Amblyseius andersoni,* which will feed on several small insect pests, larvae and eggs. The *andersoni* can be applied from shaker bottles directly on to the plants, or with the use of small distribution boxes where the bottle contents can be poured into and hung on the plants. The *andersoni* are not a direct replacement for *Encarsia,* but an additional predator to use to help establish overall control.

Encarsia formosa are supplied as black scale on cards. KOPPERT BIOLOGICAL SYSTEMS

Examples of adult whitefly on a leaf. KOPPERT BIOLOGICAL SYSTEMS

Mealybugs

Mealybugs can be a difficult pest to control in greenhouses and conservatories due to their rapid reproductive rate in the summer months and their ability to overwinter in cracks and crevices. They can hide on some plants behind leaves, within bark material and in difficult to reach locations. Mealybugs are also covered in a waxy material, which protects them from some contact-acting physical spray treatments. Mealybugs extract sap from plants, causing stunted growth and yellowing of leaves. Sticky honeydew is also produced by the mealybugs, which may lead to black mould that further disfigures the plants. There are several species that can be found in greenhouses, the common ones being the citrus mealybug and the long-tailed mealybug.

Ladybird Predators of Mealybugs

One of the ladybird species that is a specific predator of mealybugs is a species we do not see in gardens. The *Cryptolaemus montrouzieri* originates from Australia and has been used as a form of biological control against mealybugs in many countries, including on cotton crops in California. This predator can be applied in glasshouses, conservatories and interior growing areas. They do not look like normal ladybirds, having a different coloured body and head. *Cryptolaemus* beetles are supplied either as adults or in their larval form.

The easiest and most effective way to use these ladybirds for mealybug control is when they are larvae. The larvae look quite like mealybugs when in this part of their cycle, but will consume large numbers of genuine mealybugs. The larvae do not have wings at this point, so will crawl around leaves and up and down plant stems searching for mealybugs to feed on. This enables a more accurate application, as the larvae can be placed directly on to, or near, mealybug infestations before they quickly start to feed on them. In temperatures over 20°C, one *Cryptolaemus* larvae can eat over 200 mealybugs before it develops into an adult, at which point it will then continue to feed on mealybugs.

The adult *Cryptolaemus* beetle is winged and can be more difficult to apply directly to one area, as they can fly off and are attracted to light, so be careful only to introduce them to areas where windows and vents are shut for at least a few hours. This will allow the beetles time to acclimatize to their new surroundings. Adult beetles are useful if you have

Cryptolaemus larva (on the left) with mealybug. The larva of this predator can look a bit like the prey it wants to eat. PROTASOV AN/SHUTTERSTOCK.COM

very tall or inaccessible plants, as they can fly up to those higher areas.

The key to success when using *Cryptolaemus* is to ensure that temperatures are high enough and that there is plenty of day length. *Cryptolaemus* activity speeds up with warmer temperatures and they will only reproduce in longer summer days. If temperatures are below 14°C, they will not function at all. *Cryptolaemus* activity only really gets going at temperatures over 20°C, so consider carefully when and where to use them.

For large mealybug infestations, be prepared to apply relatively high numbers of *Cryptolaemus* if control is to be achieved quickly, as small introductions can prove ineffective. *Cryptolaemus* also prefer certain species of mealybugs. The reason for this is that they first like to eat the egg sacs that most mealybugs produce. The long-tailed mealybug does not produce egg sacs, so you might find that other mealybug species are eaten before the *Cryptolaemus* start to feed on the long tails.

Thrips

Thrips are the smallest winged insects and belong to an insect family called Thripidae. They are minute, pencil-shaped insects that are only a few millimetres

Long-tailed mealybugs. A persistent and difficult species of mealybug to control. WYEBUGS.CO.UK

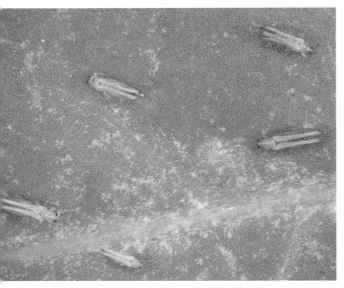

Western flower thrip adult. PROTASOV AN/SHUTTERSTOCK.COM

The larva of a western flower thrip. TOMASZ KLEJDYSZ/
SHUTTERSTOCK.COM

on leaves and flowers. Plant growth and vigour can become stunted, while fruit, such as peppers and cucumbers, can grow twisted. Thrips can also transmit viruses between plants. Both the adult thrip and larval stage will feed on plants. In warm conditions, thrip populations can double in as little as four days. The most common and damaging species of thrip is known as the western flower thrip.

Monitor and Catch

As with whitefly and other small, winged insect pests, a good starting point in your monitoring and control programmes for thrip treatment can be by the use of yellow sticky traps. These traps will help you to identify when the first thrips are present and aid in controlling the adults. This is critical, as the adult thrip has fewer natural enemies that we can apply against it. Hang the traps just above the plants' growing heads, or place on canes in plant pots.

Predatory Mites for Thrip Larvae

There are several species of predatory mites that will feed on thrip larvae, which are yellow to orange in colour. The predators are not able to feed on adult thrips, so the best strategy is to have enough predatory mites on the plants to eat sufficient thrip larvae to prevent the development of the thrip population.

The first predatory mite used for this purpose was the *Amblyseius cucumeris*. The *cucumeris* can be supplied in shaker bottles, which are then poured on to leaves for quick dispersal and application of the predators. When using shaker bottles, frequent applications can be required to maintain populations. A more cost-effective solution is to use slow-release sachets of these predatory mites. These sachets are made from paper, or more recently from foil. They contain a food source for the predatory mites, which enables them to reproduce in the sachet.

The sachets do not contain enough food to keep the predators in the sachets, however, so as their population increases they will leave the sachets and travel on to the plants, where they will search out and feed on thrip larvae. These sachets normally continue producing predators for about a month, which means that they can be introduced on to plants less frequently than shaker bottle applications. The sachets can pro-

long. Some species of thrips have become a serious problem for commercial growing under glass. Thrips are now also starting to get noticed by hobby gardeners, especially on plants grown indoors. The damage thrips can inflict on plants is out of proportion to their tiny size.

Thrips feed on plants by piercing the surface of leaves and flowers and then extracting sap and other contents. This causes silvery-grey patches to appear vide a method to maintain predatory mite populations on the plants in high enough numbers to deter and stop the build-up of thrips.

In recent years, other predatory mites have been discovered to feed on thrip larvae and some of these predators, such as the *Amblyseius swirskii*, will also feed on whitefly eggs.

Scale Insects

Scale insects are a pest that can be slow to develop but have a nasty habit of creeping up on you, where suddenly you may notice there are a lot present on your plant collections. They often appear on house plants, tropical plants, foliage plants, ferns and sometimes on outdoor shrubs and trees.

There are many different species of scale insect to try to identify, which can represent a challenge. The best way to develop a general identification and understanding of the pests, which will help you to decide which natural enemies to introduce against them, is to identify if they are armoured scales or soft scales.

Armoured Scales

This species of scale insect injects substances into the plants whilst feeding on leaves, which can turn the plants yellow or brown. In severe cases of infestation, this can kill the leaves and the plant itself. These scales do not produce honeydew, however. The scale top, or 'lid', is not attached to the insect body structure, whereas it is for soft-scale insects. It can also be quite difficult to identify the different armoured-scale species due to their similarity in appearance.

Soft Scales

Soft-scale insects do have their top, or 'lid', attached to their body and most of these species also produce large amounts of honeydew on plants, after feeding on the leaves and stems. This honeydew will often then grow black, sooty moulds, which makes plants look very messy and unattractive. Soft scales can have many generations a year and are often located on the underside of leaves and stems. Common species of the soft scales include the brown soft scale (*Coccus hesperidum*) and hemispherical scale (*Saissetia coffeae*).

Scale Insect Control in Greenhouses

At the first sign of scale insects, clean them off your plants. It is best to remove all the scale insects if possible to prevent them establishing. Try using a cloth doused with some detergent, or methylated spirits. If the scale insect numbers are too large, or the infestation is inaccessible, it will be time to consider other control methods.

Soft-scale insect, *Coccus hesperidum*. KOPPERT BIOLOGICAL SYSTEMS

Armoured-scale insect, *Diaspis boisduvalii*. ENTOCARE.NL

Biological Control of Scale Insects with Natural Enemies

Armoured Scales

Some predatory beetles from the ladybird family can be introduced to feed on armoured-scale insects. The most commonly applied predator in the UK is called the *Chilocorus nigritus*. This black-coloured predatory beetle will punch a hole in the scale and eat its insides. This predator does require quite high temperatures to be active, however, with an optimum temperature of approximately 22°C, and also prefers relatively high humidity. There is a similar predatory beetle, called the *Rhyzobius lophanthae*, which will also feed on armoured scales. These beetles will operate at slightly lower temperatures than the *Chilocorus* and will also tolerate a lower humidity. Both insects are more suited to introductions in the spring and summer months, when day lengths and temperatures are higher. The optimum application period therefore should be between March and September, and in the evenings when windows and doors are shut.

There is also a parasitic wasp that will attack the *Pinnaspis aspidistrae* and *Diaspis boisduvalii* armoured scales called the *Encarsia citrina*. This is a different species to the *Encarsia* used against whitefly and is utilized by some botanical gardens. It can be a little expensive, however, for use by a hobby gardener.

Soft Scales

Controlling soft scales in the UK with natural enemies is difficult simply due to the scarcity of parasites or

Rhyzobius lophantae, a predatory beetle of scale insects.
ENTOCARE.NL

predators available that can be used in the UK against these pests. Most of the known natural enemies are not native to the UK and do not yet have release licences authorized from the UK government, while the few that can be applied are not produced by many commercial insect producers.

One parasitic wasp that was previously available was the *Metaphycus helvolus*, which is a tiny parasite that lays its egg in several soft-scale species. The hatched parasite then eats its way out of the scale, killing it. A small exit hole can be observed on the scale when these parasites are present. Sometimes these wasps can occur in greenhouses naturally, so check your scales with a magnifying glass to identify their presence. If these parasitic wasps do become available again, they should be introduced into greenhouses from spring to early autumn (March to October in the UK).

A final potential scale insect predator to mention is the mealybug predator, the *Cryptolaemus*, which will also feed on soft-scale insects when they have finished eating the mealybugs. So, if the *Cryptolaemus* have been introduced specifically for mealybug control, there may also be a welcome side effect if the predators feed on available scale insects too.

If no natural enemies are available for soft-scale control, or the temperatures are too low to permit their application, other methods of control should be considered. Some 'safe' or 'physical acting' sprays can have an impact in killing scale insects. These products do not contain poisons but ingredients, such as fatty acids,

Chilocorus nigritus, a predatory beetle of scale insects.
ENTOCARE.NL

Metaphycus, a parasitic wasp
of soft-scale insects.
ENTOCARE.NL

Cryptolaemus larvae feeding on scale insect at Cambridge
University Botanic Garden. COURTESY OF ALEX SUMMERS

that suffocate pests in a physical mode of action. They leave no harmful residues on plants that may kill future introductions of beneficial insects. If these sprays are used in a targeted way against soft scales, they will slow down their development and aid the process of manually cleaning the scales from the plants.

Other Greenhouse Pests and Principles of Biological Pest Control in Greenhouses

It is not possible to cover all the insect pests that may arrive or occur in glasshouses in this book. There are leaf hoppers, leaf miners, tortrix moths and many others, for instance, that I have not yet referred to in detail. Some of these insects do have accessible natural enemies that can be purchased and applied, whereas others are too minor and therefore do not. If no controls are available, physical removal of the pest or infected plants may be the only answer. The key to insect pest control in greenhouses is to start clean and finish clean. Try not to carry over insect pest populations from one year to the next and start introductions of natural enemies as soon as temperatures and conditions permit. Delaying introductions, especially with rapidly developing pests like greenfly, aphids and spider mite, can lead to failures and higher costs.

CHAPTER 6

VEGETABLE PESTS AND THEIR NATURAL ENEMIES

Outdoors is a far more challenging environment in which to control insect pests using natural enemies. This can be explained by numerous factors; for one there, are no small, confined areas where conditions can be manipulated, such as with heating or with the introduction of high numbers of beneficial insects into those areas for maximum impact. It can also be very expensive to release large numbers of natural enemies over wide areas, when compared to smaller greenhouse spaces.

Biological control outdoors, although successful in some areas, is less commonly used than in greenhouses and this is mainly due to knowledge gaps and limited availability of natural enemies to utilize in outdoor environments. This is changing gradually, however, especially for hobby growers and gardeners who have so few insecticides to choose from. Solutions are needed, and most gardeners prefer natural ones.

Physical protection of plants can be a good starting point when establishing a pest control programme outdoors. If you are propagating your own plants, make sure that the propagating area is kept pest-free, as was encouraged earlier, in Chapter 4. Some pests can also be kept at bay with fleeces and netting, but these are not foolproof and often have to be removed when plants are larger, or when air circulation is required to prevent diseases. One of the more successful groups of natural enemies used outside are nematodes and it is with the nematodes we start, as we look at slug control for vegetables.

Slugs and Snails

Slugs and snails, especially slugs, can be very destructive pests in wet climates such as we have in the UK. Slugs will consume huge amounts of leaf area and plants, and young plants can be completely wiped out by slugs. Crops, such as potatoes, may look healthy on the surface, but underneath the soil small slugs may be chewing their way through potato tubers, leaving holes and making the potatoes inedible. On the surface, tell-tale signs such as slime trails will reveal where slugs have been active. Brassicas and vegetables are a favourite food source for slugs, and leaves can often show large areas of ragged damage. Slugs will be active both beneath and above the soil. Some larger species of slug, in fact, can be quite useful for consuming decaying old plant matter, but most gardeners would rather not have them.

Slug damage on potatoes can be devastating. VLADKK/SHUTTERSTOCK.COM

Snails are surface feeders and generally not as destructive as slugs, but can be a problem in large numbers. There are a huge variety of anti-slug and snail products available to the gardener, with many products offering varying degrees of success. Some products rely on providing physical barriers to prevent slugs and snails reaching their plant targets. They can be successful for a while. but have shortcomings. Copper-based barriers can be effective when they are clean, as they give the slug or snail a static electric shock, which deters them from travelling over the surface of the copper. There are copper rings available for placing around plants or copper tape that can be applied to pots to prevent the slugs and snails getting to the plants. They become less effective with time, however, as they become dirty and if the slug or snail is already in the pot, they can trap them just where they are not wanted! There are other physical barriers available such as sharp grit or even sheep wool, which can help deter, but does not reduce, the slug and snail population.

There are also traps available, such as pitfall traps, which are dug into the soil with a bait added, such as beer. The slugs and snails fall into these traps and are captured or instantly die. The traps can catch quite high numbers. but are not selective, so beneficial insects, such as some beetle species, will also be caught. These traps therefore sometimes have the undesired effect of reducing the natural population of beneficial insects that do feed on slugs.

Slug Pellets

Slug pellets have a bad name and, in most cases, justifiably. Many pellets have contained very harmful insecticide baits, which killed not only slugs, but harmed wildlife by poisoning frogs, toads and hedgehogs; the very wildlife that helps to naturally control slugs and snails in our gardens. Thankfully, most of the harmful ones have been withdrawn from sale in the UK. There are some iron-based pellets (ferric phosphate), which are still available and can be quite

Snails in large numbers can cause serious damage to plants. PITTAWUT/ SHUTTERSTOCK.COM

Ferrimax slug pellets are ferric phosphate-based, so are safe to wildlife.

effective in controlling slugs and snails. They do not have the harmful side effects of the previous insecticide-based pellets. However, all pellets are limited in their effectiveness, as, firstly, they are not mobile and rely on the slug and snail coming into contact with them; and, secondly, they tend to degrade quite quickly, especially in wet weather. What is needed is a more mobile control that will grow in numbers, and this is what we now have with slug-killing nematodes.

Slug Nematodes

Phasmarhabditis hermaphrodita nematodes were researched and developed by the Long Ashton Research Station in the 1990s, before being developed as a commercial product that gardeners and growers could use. This naturally occurring nematode is already present in some slugs, but not normally in enough numbers to kill the slug. Applying higher numbers, with a purchased pack of slug nematodes, is an effective method for controlling certain slug species and particularly those that attack plants underground, such as potatoes.

Surface-feeding slugs and snails are not controlled very effectively with slug nematodes, as it is not easy to get the nematodes into contact with them. Like most

Slugs will expand, especially around the neck area, when infected with nematodes. BASF NEMASYS WEBSITE

nematode species, after application the population will fall back or decline once the slug numbers decline, so further applications may be required if slug numbers start to rise again. Slug nematodes require a minimum soil temperature of 5°C and must not be applied in freezing conditions; early spring applications can therefore have varying results if the weather is cold. As with all nematode applications, slug nematodes must be applied with plenty of water.

Caterpillars

There are many species of caterpillar that like to feed on vegetables, but perhaps the most harmful are the caterpillars of cabbage white butterflies, which can cause significant damage to brassica plants. Covering the plants with netting will help to protect them, but if the butterflies get underneath the netting, they will very soon lay eggs that develop into hungry caterpillars. Few gardeners want to spray insecticides on to plants they wish to eat, so a more natural solution is required.

Commercial growers have access to a natural bacterium called *Bacillus thuringiensis*, which is safe to

Large white caterpillar. A very damaging pest to brassica plants.

use on edible plants and causes no harm to wildlife, other than caterpillars. Unfortunately, there is no legal version of the product available in the UK for hobby use, as the licence for its use expired some years ago. This has led to research into which natural enemies could be used against caterpillars. There is ongoing work into identifying tiny parasitic wasps with which to infect moth and butterfly eggs. These products may become available for outdoor use in the UK in the future. Some countries even release the parasites using drones to apply them to large-scale areas. For now, however, we are looking at nematodes to provide a solution.

Most nematodes used to be solely applied to the ground or soil, but some species can now be applied above ground, directly on to the target pest, which is in this case the caterpillar. The nematode species that survives the longest on the leaf is the *Steinernema carpocapsae*. If the caterpillars can be identified and are accessible, the nematodes can be sprayed directly on to them. Choose an overcast, warm and damp day if possible. The moisture and warmth will help the nematodes to remain active for long enough to penetrate and kill the caterpillars. The nematodes will not survive long on the plants, so any fresh infestations of caterpillars will require further applications. These nematodes are practically invisible and are harmless to humans and wildlife.

Aphids

Aphids can quickly turn the most appealing vegetables into sickly looking, sticky plants covered in honeydew and mould, which look far from appetizing. Aphids also stunt plant growth, leading to reduced yields. There are several species of aphid that can often be found on vegetable plots and allotments, including the black bean aphid on beans, which is also often found on nasturtiums and dahlias. An aphid species often found on brassicas is the mealy cabbage aphid, which forms in clusters of grey-white colonies on the underside of brassica leaves. Both species of aphids, and others, can go unnoticed for some time, so it is important to check plants on a regular basis, rather than wait for large numbers to build up.

As with other pests on edible plants, spraying a poison-based control on the plants is not desirable. A further advantage of not using chemical insecticides is that many naturally occurring predators and parasites will soon appear, such as hoverflies, lacewings and ladybirds. Sometimes these natural populations of predators do not appear quickly enough to prevent damage to plants, so the natural levels of predators can be introduced or topped up prior to the natural population appearing.

Aphids can reproduce very quickly in huge numbers. FLOKI/ SHUTTERSTOCK.COM

Aulacorthum solani aphid species. KOPPERT BIOLOGICAL SYSTEMS

Myzus persicae var persicae aphid species. KOPPERT BIOLOGICAL SYSTEMS

Topping Up Your Natural Predator Levels

Choosing which predator can depend on the growing habit of the vegetable or salads concerned. If there are aphids present on low-growing plants with plenty of leaf surface, such as lettuces or cabbages, a good option is to apply lacewing larvae by shaking out the predators from the shaker bottle over the leaf surface. These tiny voracious predatory larvae will crawl over the foliage, consuming large numbers of aphids. The larvae are nocturnal, though, so can be difficult to observe in action during the day. Only apply the lacewing larvae when aphids are present on the plants. It may take more than one application of lacewings to reduce the aphid population to a safe level.

For difficult to reach areas of plants, for instance with black bean aphids located high up on runner beans, it is not easy to apply lots of tiny lacewing larvae from a bottle, so consider instead using ladybird larvae.

The ladybird larvae can be applied by emptying their transport bottle or container into a jute or cotton bag, which can then be hung higher on the plants near the aphids. The larvae then exit the bags to locate and consume the aphids. These larvae can eat many aphids and have the advantage of developing into adults that will continue to feed on the aphids.

Carrot Root Flies

Carrot root fly (*Psila rosae*) attack carrots, parsnips, parsley and even celery. The adult carrot root flies will lay their eggs near such plants. These eggs will then develop into creamy-yellow larvae that tunnel into the carrots, disfiguring them and enabling diseases and rots to get inside the carrots. Signs of carrot root fly activity are clear from blueish-purple foliage showing.

For many years, the only solution was covering the carrots with fleece to hide and protect them from the carrot root flies and therefore also reduce their egg laying. This is still good practice, but once the fleece is removed the carrots can still be vulnerable to egg laying from the adult flies. It is also possible that overwintering carrot root fly larvae and pupae could emerge under the fleece in the spring. What is required instead is a biological control solution that can be applied to the soil at the time the carrot root fly larvae are present in the soil. This can be provided by applications of nematodes that kill carrot root fly larvae.

A typical ladybird larvae application bag, which helps to apply the ladybirds in difficult to reach spots.

Carrot root fly. The adult fly lays eggs that turn into harmful larvae. DRAGONFLI.CO.UK

Carrot root fly larva. The larva of a carrot root fly can be killed with nematodes. DRAGONFLI. CO.UK

This carrot root fly sticky trap has an angled design to catch carrot root flies and not other insects. KOPPERT BIOLOGICAL SYSTEMS

Nematodes for the Control of Carrot Root Fly Larvae

Spring-grown carrots will be developing in April and May and this is a time when the soil becomes warm enough for the application of nematodes. Some of the species of nematodes used against pests, such as leatherjackets and vine weevil, have also been shown to attack and control carrot root fly larvae, especially nematodes of the *Steinernema* species. These nematodes provide another chemical pesticide-free solution to a very damaging pest. They should be applied from April onwards until harvesting, and again later in the summer for second crops of carrots.

You can also place orange carrot root fly traps near the carrots. These traps will catch the adult flies and offer advance warning that eggs are being laid which will develop into the damaging larvae. Once the adult carrot root fly is observed on the traps, you may wish to begin considering the application of nematodes. These are applied by watering them in the soil around the carrots. Ensure that the soil is moist at time of application and keep the soil moist for at least a week to aid the passage of the nematodes through the soil. The nematodes can be watered in using a watering can or some hose-end feeders. A repeat application will be needed for each generation of carrot root fly.

The larva of a turnip moth; cutworms are normally found in the soil. BLACKTHORN ARABLE/SHUTTERSTOCK.COM

Cutworms

Cutworms are the soil-dwelling larvae or caterpillar stage of several moth species, including turnip moths (*Agrotis segetum*). An indication of their presence is the appearance of plants that appear to wilt and then die. This is due to the roots of such plants being fed on by these brownish-green caterpillars in the soil. They will also sometimes feed on the surface at night, which can result in the tops of plants being cut off as they feed on the stems.

Nematodes for Cutworm Control

Again, our old friend, the *Steinernema* species of nematode can be deployed, this time against this soil-dwelling pest. Once damage to plants is observed, or the caterpillars are found in the soil, water in the cutworm-killing nematodes. The nematodes will move through the soil to infect and kill the cutworms. Cutworm activity occurs during the summer months, which is also the best season for nematode applications, if the soil is moist at the time of application. If the soil is not moist, irrigate or water the soil prior to use.

New Biological Controls for Vegetable Pests

Biological control for produce grown outside is not as commonly available as it is for indoor-grown produce. This is evolving, however, as new techniques are constantly being tested. Two of the latest forms of biological control for outside produce are detailed below.

Cabbage/Brassica Whiteflies

Brassica plants, like cabbage, sprouts and kale, can suffer from large infestations of the brassica whitefly pest, resulting in a sticky mess on the plant with growing black moulds. This form of whitefly is not the same species as the glasshouse whitefly, which we can control indoors with tiny parasites. This whitefly requires a more robust natural enemy that can act at a lower temperature. Some predatory mites that are used for thrip control have also been observed feeding on the eggs of this whitefly, and tests and trials are now under way to evaluate their effectiveness against brassica whitefly.

Asparagus Beetles

Adults and larvae of asparagus beetle feed on asparagus plants, causing severe damage and reduction in yield from the plants. Work carried out by Koppert Biological Systems in France has shown that nematode applications to the larval stage of the beetle, while it is feeding on the plant, kills many of the larvae. This will then have an impact on reducing the overall beetle population. Asparagus beetles have two generations a year and their larvae can

Brassica cabbage whitefly. A different species to glasshouse whitefly that requires different biological controls. A.J. CESPEDES/SHUTTERSTOCK.COM

Asparagus beetle. An attractive but damaging beetle species. IAN REDDING/SHUTTERSTOCK.COM

Asparagus beetle larvae. This is the stage of the asparagus life cycle that nematodes can control. IAN REDDING/SHUTTERSTOCK.COM

normally be found on plants in the UK in May and June, and then again in August and September. It is especially important to treat the late summer generation to prevent them overwintering and causing problems the following year. Some UK nematode suppliers are now selling nematodes for asparagus beetle control.

Other pests that are currently being examined for control using nematodes include the cabbage root fly and wireworms. Trials by professional growers and gardeners are under way to establish which species of nematodes might provide a control for these pests. The established data and information are not quite confirmed yet, but one can expect nematode-based products for such pests to become available in the near future.

CHAPTER 7

FRUIT PESTS AND THEIR NATURAL ENEMIES

Fruit and the relevant pests that target them, like vegetables in the previous chapter, are a big category to cover. Therefore, I shall narrow it down by splitting the pests' categories into those of soft fruit pests, which attack plants like strawberries, raspberries and gooseberries; and the top fruit pests, which attack the fruit trees of apples, pears and cherries.

Soft Fruit Pests and their Natural Enemies

Vine Weevils

Strawberries can be susceptible to several insect pests, especially if grown in greenhouses or polythene tunnels. One of the most destructive pests is that of the vine weevil. Their larvae, which are cream coloured with a brown head, feed on the roots of strawberry plants. Strawberry plants growing in pots or growbags can suddenly look like they have not been watered and appear to wilt, but on closer inspection it is often the case that most of the root system has been eaten or damaged, which can be fatal to the plant.

The confined environment of a pot or growbag provides the ideal conditions for the vine weevil larvae to prosper. These conditions do, though, also provide a suitable environment for the application of nematodes that will kill these pests' larvae. If you discover vine weevil larvae in the compost or soil, quickly apply some nematodes directly to the infected pots or growbags, or to open beds if growing outside. The nematodes need to be watered in thoroughly and the growing media kept moist for about a week. During this period, the nematodes will search out and kill the larvae. This can be difficult to observe, as it is occurring beneath the surface. The vine weevil larvae will turn brown once infected and most of the larvae will die within a week of the nematode application.

It is possible to use these nematodes as a preventative measure by applying them once a month when the plants are growing. They should be applied early in the plants' life, when the plants need to gain a lot of root growth, so are vulnerable to damage from vine weevil larvae. By applying the nematodes on a regular basis, a population of nematodes will remain live and active in the growing media ready to kill any freshly hatched larvae.

Vine weevil larvae. These larvae can destroy plant roots, leading to plant death. KOPPERT BIOLOGICAL SYSTEMS

Red Spider Mites

The other major insect pest that is a threat to strawberry plants are harmful mites, such as the red spider mite; although in greenhouses, there can be also issues with thrips and aphids. The spider mite that is most common on strawberries is the two-spotted mite (*Tetranychus urticae*). The mites feed on the leaves, turning them yellow, and in high numbers can cause webbing on the plants. In such high numbers, they weaken plants, stunting growth and yield. To emphasize how fast they can reproduce in warm conditions, the spider mite population can double within three days!

There are several predatory mites that can be introduced to protect plants from spider mite, but for the hobby gardener the best choice is *Phytoseiulus persimilis*. The *persimilis* should be utilized as soon as spider mites are observed. These tiny *persimilis* mites move quicker and reproduce faster than spider mites and will succeed in quickly reducing and controlling spider mite populations. They are applied with a shaker bottle directly on to the leaves where the spider mite is present. By looking carefully, or using a hand lens, the *persimilis* can be observed on plants, feeding on spider mites and moving over leaves searching for their prey.

If conditions are warm enough, *persimilis* can be used on indoor- or outdoor-grown strawberries; temperatures need to be over 15°C to allow for their use. Try to apply these predators before the spider mite are making webs, as the webs may already contain thou-

sands of spider mites, which may require multiple applications of predators to control. Early identification of the spider mite population is vital.

Raspberry Beetles

The raspberry beetle (*Byturus tomentosus*) is a small grey-brown beetle. It lays eggs on the raspberry flowers in early and midsummer. These eggs develop into creamy white larvae/grubs that eat soft fruit such as raspberries, blackberries, loganberries and tayberries. The grubs feed on the stalk of the fruit and then move inside the fruit to eat. Infected fruit plants can be identified by their grey-brown stalks. In the autumn, the grubs will turn into pupae that drop on to the soil beneath the plants. It is at this stage that we can encourage some naturally occurring predators, such as birds and ground beetles, to feed on the pupae, by disturbing the soil in the autumn and spring. There are not yet any natural enemies that we can introduce to supplement this natural control, so we are only left with the option of trying to catch and trap some of the beetles, which can be achieved with the raspberry beetle trap.

Raspberry beetle traps are designed to attract raspberry beetles. They incorporate two features that help this happen; an attractant lure to attract the beetles in and white-coloured vanes to mimic raspberry flowers. The attractant lure is not based on a sex pheromone like many traps, but is a floral attractant that entices the beetles to the trap. The beetles fly to the trap, hit the white vanes, then drop down into the collection section of the bucket. Place the trap in or near where your raspberry canes are planted and make sure that it has

Spider mites on strawberry plants can cause extensive damage. CATHERINE ECKERT/SHUTTERSTOCK.COM

This raspberry beetle trap attracts the adult raspberry beetle with an attractant scent.

an active attractant lure from April to catch the first emerging beetles.

Gooseberry Sawflies

There are several species of gooseberry sawfly that can attack gooseberries and some currants. It is the larval stage of the gooseberry sawfly life cycle that will do the damage. The larvae of the sawfly look like caterpillars and are green with black spots. These hungry larvae can shred and defoliate gooseberry bushes rapidly. They can be found on plants from April to September in the UK. As with most edible fruit and plants, the prospect of applying an insecticide is not a good solution.

Until quite recently, a natural option was quite difficult to achieve, but there is now a nematode-based solution. Gooseberry sawfly larvae can be sprayed with *Steinernema carpocapsae* nematodes. As with other leaf or foliage applications of nematodes, it is important to apply them only when the larvae are present and not on bright days. Ideally, choose a damp,

warm day for application and spray the nematode solution directly on to the gooseberry sawfly larvae.

New Pest of Soft Fruit

A new invader and pest species of soft fruits is a fruit fly that has reached the UK. The spotted-wing drosophila (*Drosophila suzukii*), often referred to as SWD, originated from Asia and lays its eggs under the skin of fruit. These eggs then develop into larvae that feed in the

Gooseberry sawfly larva – these look like caterpillars and can be controlled with nematodes. HEITI PAVES/ SHUTTERSTOCK.COM

Drosophila suzukii fruit fly. A new non-native pest of soft fruit in the UK. TOMASZ KLEJDYSZ/SHUTTERSTOCK.COM

fruit, causing the fruit to collapse. The larvae can target strawberries, raspberries, blueberries, currants, plums, cherries and even grapes.

To date, there are no natural enemies at our disposal to use against this pest. There are SWD traps, which can be purchased to hang on plants and catch and trap adult SWD flies. There are also some companies producing fine insect netting that can cover plants to protect them from the adult flies. The fruit-growing sector is very keen to find a natural solution to this new invasive and highly damaging fruit pest.

Top Fruit Pests

There is a fruit tree red spider mite that can arrive on top fruit. The leaves of apples and plums will turn yellow and dark coloured if mites appear on the leaves. In high numbers, this can lead to early leaf fall, but generally this spider mite does not cause as many problems as the two-spotted mite does on soft fruit. The predatory mite *Amblyseius andersoni* can also be applied to trees as a treatment against this mite. The more serious pests for fruit trees are moth-related.

Codling Moths

Apples and pears can be targeted by codling moths (*Cydia pomonella*). These moths are not a pest problem at their adult stage, but are so in their larval, or caterpillar, form, when they can cause serious damage to fruit. Small white caterpillars will tunnel inside the fruit and eat the core. They will then leave an exit hole on the outside of the fruit, which makes the fruit unattractive and inedible. Adult codling moths are active in the UK from May to July and will lay their eggs on developing fruit. Some organic growers in Europe are applying tiny egg parasites in the form of *Trichogramma* wasps to try to prevent the moth eggs from developing and this may also become an option in the UK as soon as a native species is identified and bred. For now, the first step to reduce and control the damage from this moth is to apply the use of pheromone traps.

Codling moth pheromone traps should be put out from May to attract and catch male codling moths with a pheromone sex lure. This helps to reduce the numbers of males available to mate and indirectly leads to less egg laying. The use of pheromone traps is not a control, but can be used as part of a strategy to reduce

Spider mite often goes unnoticed on top fruit and does have natural predators in nature.
V. PALES/
SHUTTERSTOCK.COM

numbers. Most average-sized gardens will only require one codling moth pheromone trap. It is important to make sure that the pheromone lure is fresh and active. Most lures will last at least six weeks and there are long-life pheromone lures available that can last for up to sixteen weeks.

If codling moth eggs do hatch and the larvae burrow into the fruit, unfortunately there is very little that can be done to treat them once they are already there. The next stage in the biological or natural control pro-gramme should be the use of nematodes on the codling moth larvae when they are on the tree trunk and branches.

Plum Fruit Moths

Plum fruit moths (*Grapholita funebrana*) produce a pink-coloured caterpillar with a brown head that feeds inside ripening fruit. They can appear in plums, dam-sons and gages. Once the caterpillars are feeding inside the fruit, they leave grey excrement pellets in the fruit and infected fruit can also ripen early. The plum fruit moth usually has one generation a year and adult moths are active from May onwards.

The use of pheromone traps is important as part of a strategy to reduce this moth species. Place plum fruit pheromone traps out in trees from May. The phero-mone in these traps is quite powerful, so you do not need to hang out many traps. One trap will normally provide enough pheromone to cover at least twelve trees. Setting up too many traps can produce too much pheromone, which can negate the effectiveness of the traps' catch rate of male plum fruit moths. The pheromone traps will not catch all the males and they do not catch the females. The traps will, however, pro-vide advance warning of moth activity and help to reduce the number of males mating with females, which should reduce egg laying.

Using Nematodes Against Fruit Tree Pests

Codling moth larvae and plum fruit larvae can be treated with nematodes when they are on the fruit

Codling moth larva is difficult to treat once inside apples and pears. CH. WEISS/SHUTTERSTOCK. COM

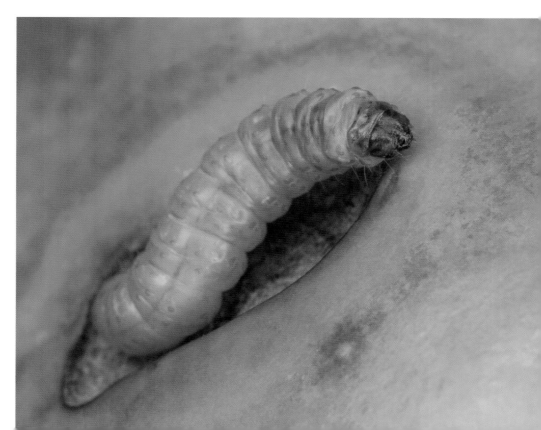

Codling moth larva in an apple. DIMID_86 / SHUTTERSTOCK.COM

Plum fruit larvae. OFF5173/ SHUTTERSTOCK.COM

tree trunks and branches. This occurs two times a year; when the moths are coming out from overwintering in the spring (April) and again just before they overwinter (September–October). This is a unique way to use and apply nematodes. It can be difficult to observe the larvae, as they will sometimes hide in crevices and bark. The tree trunk and branches should therefore be thoroughly sprayed with nematode solution to get the nematodes on to the larvae. Some larvae may also fall to the ground and overwinter in the soil or debris on the floor, so drenching the soil at the base of the trees is also good practice.

By applying nematodes with this method, the larval population of the codling moth and plum fruit moth can be reduced before the moths overwinter and those that do overwinter can be treated in the spring. It is unlikely that 100 per cent of the larvae will be killed, but the nematodes will certainly reduce the population and help to form part of a wider strategy to cull the overall population.

Other Fruit Pests

There are plenty of other pests of fruit to watch out for, but these are generally more minor pests. There are aphid pests such as the cherry blackfly, for instance, which cause leaf curl and browning leaves, but most healthy cherry trees should not be impacted by this pest. If very high numbers of aphids appear, natural predator levels can be boosted with the added application of ladybird larvae. There are also other moths, such as the winter moth, where the adults are active later in the season. Their caterpillars eat blossom and can damage forming fruit, but do not normally appear in high enough numbers to warrant treatment.

If growing soft fruit indoors, many of the pests that attack salads and ornamental plants may transfer to fruit plants, so be aware of this and use sticky traps to monitor such pests as aphids, whitefly and thrips. Fruit pests, like other pests, need monitoring constantly and some forethought and planning is required with the use of pheromone traps to detect damaging moth species.

CHAPTER 8

LAWN PESTS AND THEIR NATURAL ENEMIES

The withdrawal from sale of insecticides to control turf and lawn pests has had a big impact on gardeners and those that manage sports turf and amenity areas. Many hobby and professional gardeners previously relied on a small number of chemical-based insecticides to supress lawn insect pests and these products are no longer available. For the environment, this is a good-news story with no more possible side effects on earthworms, pollinators and other beneficial organisms.

Some pests, however, are now more visible than before. Their presence in lawns often leads to secondary damage that is caused by animals and birds searching for these very insects to feed on. For example, if there are large numbers of crows on grass areas, this often denotes a high presence of leatherjacket larvae. If badgers are in the local neighbourhood, they are quite capable of destroying lawns looking for chafer grubs to eat. It is also not just gardens where these extra visitors appear, but golf courses, playing fields, parks and even racecourses. The damage from animals and birds looking for turf pests can cause more damage than the insect pest itself.

There are two major lawn pests, plus a small number of minor ones. In this chapter, we will focus on the two

major pests and how to control them through the use of nematodes.

Chafer Grubs

Chafer grubs are the larvae of the beetle family *Scarabaeidae*. The adult beetles feed on leaves and flowers, but the damage is not normally noticed or observed. It is the grub stage of the life cycle that causes the most problems. There are several species of chafer beetle native to the UK, with the garden chafer (*Phyllopertha horticola*) the more common of the varying species. The adults are a brown colour with a green and black head and neck, and they emerge from the soil and lawns in May and June. Sometimes, the garden chafers emerge in such high numbers that they create a low-flying swarm of beetles.

The females feed for a few days, mate, then lay eggs. Each female can lay about thirty eggs and these eggs hatch within three to four weeks, after which they become the chafer grubs. These larvae quickly start to feed on the grass roots and can create yellowing areas of lawns where the roots are being weakened and consumed. In severe infestations, grass can be pulled up with no roots attached. When temperatures start to lower in the soil during the autumn, the larger chafer grub larvae stop feeding and move deeper into the soil structure. It is here that they overwinter and hibernate, going as deep as 50 cm (20 in). The following spring, they rise to the surface to pupate in March–April. This is when they begin the process of turning into a beetle; at this point the pupae are coloured cream to brown.

Secondary Damage

Even worse than the yellowing lawns caused by the chafer grubs is the secondary damage that can be caused by birds and animals. Chafer grubs are a tempting food source for animals, especially badgers. These largely nocturnal animals detect the grubs under the grass surface and will pull back layers of turf to get to the grubs underneath. This can cause enormous damage to lawn areas.

Natural Control of Chafers with Traps and Nematodes

Chafer beetles can be caught in high numbers with the use of garden chafer traps, if they are placed out near, or on, lawns at the right time. The chafer beetles normally emerge in May–June, so make sure that traps are in place for this period. The beetles often make for flower beds, borders and shrubs in which to feed and mate, so placing traps in these areas is advisable. The beetles also fly at quite a low level, so do not hang the traps up too high. Garden chafer traps use a floral attractant, rather than being pheromone-based, which means they will catch both males and females.

Even with a high catch rate of beetles, it is unlikely that enough females will be caught to prevent egg laying, but the population can be reduced and the traps can provide an early warning signal that chafer grubs are likely to appear a few months later. To control

Chafer grubs – the larval stage of Chafer beetles. STEPHEN FARHALL/SHUTTERSTOCK.COM

Chafer grub damage and badger damage to lawns.

the grubs, the solution comes in the form of nematodes.

Nematode treatments against chafer grub are the only control treatment available to UK gardeners. The level of control with nematodes can vary and several factors will influence the success rate, such as the nematode species, the timing of the application, the climate and the soil structure. All of these factors, except for perhaps the soil structure, can be influenced by the gardener. Nematode treatments against chafers are always applied to the soil through the grass thatch.

Nematode Species

In the UK, all the main suppliers of chafer grub control nematodes sell the *Heterorhabditis* species. This species, under the appropriate conditions, provides the highest kill rate of chafer grubs of all the nematode species available to gardeners. It does, however, require a soil temperature of at least 13°C to be active, although this should not be a problem in the summer months when the nematodes are applied.

Timing of Applications and the Chafer Grub Life Cycle

The timing of the application, or applications, is imperative. Chafer grubs start to appear under lawns from the end of July. Nematode treatments are more

Chafer trap – an attractant- based trap for chafer beetles.

Nematode-infected chafer grubs; the grubs will eventually disintegrate.

effective against the grubs when they are small, so early August is the best time for application, if the chafer grubs are present. The best way to check if this is the case is to dig up a few small areas of turf, especially in yellowing areas of the lawn, and identify the white-coloured chafer grubs in the soil. Once you are sure the grubs are present, begin your application of the nematode treatment.

Applications can be made from the end of July until the end of October, but earlier applications tend to be more effective. Chafer grubs that survive the summer will overwinter in the soil and remain dormant until the following spring. The soil will be too cold, however, for applications of *Heterorhabditis* species nematodes at that point. This makes a successful application of nematodes in the summer period even more significant.

Irrigation and Watering

For the nematodes to be able to penetrate the grass thatch and soil surface, moisture is very important. If the nematodes are applied to rock-hard soil with little water, they will be unable to reach the chafer grubs and will die on the soil surface. Professional turf managers now often apply soil penetrants and spreaders along with the nematodes to aid their passage into the soil. If using such products, it is important to know if they are compatible with the nematodes. Some online suppliers of nematodes to gardeners also offer these products.

The most important factor to remember is to apply the nematodes with plenty of water. It is good practice to irrigate and water the lawn prior to application of the nematodes and keep the lawn moist for about a week afterwards. Spiking the lawn prior to applications will also aid the passage of water and nematodes into the soil. If the weather patterns permit, choose a damp, overcast day for application. The nematodes can be applied with watering cans for smaller lawns. For larger lawns, sprayers can be used, or certain types of hose-end feeders that can be fixed on to a hosepipe. These provide a much quicker method of applying the nematodes over larger areas. It should be noted that nematodes are UV sensitive, so do not thrive in hot, sunny, dry conditions.

Soil Type and Structure

The type of soil you have can also influence how successful your nematode applications will be. If it is a very sandy soil, both water and nematodes will soak in well, although sometimes too quickly and the nematodes may be washed through the soil. If you have a very heavy clay soil, this can make passage of the nematodes slightly more difficult through the soil due to its density. Either of these conditions may require more applications of nematodes than if treating more general soil.

Nematodes applied with a hose-end feeder – a faster way to apply them to larger lawns.

Number of Applications Required

Nematodes are rarely capable of killing all the grubs they are applied against. The ideal scenario is for the nematodes to kill a high percentage of the grubs, so that the numbers left do not attract birds and animals to dig them up or cause large areas of root death. Healthy lawns with good root growth can normally sustain low numbers of chafer grubs. It can be difficult to judge how effective an application of nematodes has been. One obvious sign is a decline in bird and animal activity on the lawn, while another indicator can be provided by digging up a small piece of turf and seeing what is alive underneath. It can be difficult to spot fully infected grubs, as they tend to go dark coloured and eventually explode underground! This also has the effect of releasing more nematodes into the surrounding area.

Some lawns can be subject to very high numbers of grubs, with the result that even with a 70 per cent kill ratio achieved with nematodes, there might still be quite large amounts of grubs remaining. For lawns with large infestations, it is sensible to apply more than one application of nematodes. Try two applications with an interval of two weeks. Some gardens may require successive years of nematode applications to reduce chafer grub numbers, or, if treating an area of high chafer beetle activity, annual applications may be required.

Leatherjackets

Leatherjackets are the larvae of the crane fly. They belong to the *Tipula spp* family and can be active from February to October in the UK. The larvae are a grey to brown colour and, like chafer grubs, feed mainly on grass roots. They can sometimes be found eating seedlings or located within flower beds.

The adults, which most gardeners know as daddy long-legs, lay their eggs in lawns from August to October and can often be observed in high numbers on lawns during this period. The eggs quickly develop into the leatherjacket larvae that will begin feeding on grass roots. The damage is very similar to that of chafer grubs, with the results showing as yellowing areas of grass on lawns. Birds, such as starlings and crows, especially enjoy feeding on the leatherjackets and will peck lawns, digging them up for food. This secondary damage can be very destructive to lawns.

To find out whether you have leatherjackets, you can dig up a small piece of turf in an area where there is clear damage. Alternatively, you can water an area and place a piece of black polythene over it at night, which will draw the larvae up to the surface where they can be identified. Leatherjacket larvae will feed on lawns from late August until the end of October, and sometimes a bit later if there are mild conditions. They will also sink down in the soil structure, like chafer grubs, in the cold winter months and remain dormant. If there is a wet, mild winter, however, they can be found feeding on the surface as early as February.

Biological Pest Control of Leatherjackets

There are currently no trapping products available to catch the adult crane fly/daddy long-legs, so the control of these insects is entirely based on successful

Leatherjacket larva – the larva of a daddy longlegs (crane fly). EDWIN BUTTER/SHUTTERSTOCK.COM

nematode applications. Many of the factors referred to when detailing the application of chafer-control nematodes earlier in this chapter also apply to the application process for the control of leatherjackets. One difference, however, is the species of nematodes used. Leatherjackets can be controlled with two species: either the *Steinernema feltiae*, or the *Steinernema carpocapsae*. Both species will attack the leatherjackets. *Steinernema feltiae* will be active at slightly lower soil temperatures (from 10°C) than the *Steinernema carpocapsae* (from 12°C). All of the other application factors and requirements are the same as those mentioned for chafer control, that is, plenty of irrigation and application on warm, damp, overcast days.

Timing of Leatherjacket Nematode Applications

Leatherjacket larvae can be active in the early spring and there is a temptation to apply nematodes against these overwintered leatherjackets. The success of early spring applications of nematodes, however, can be limited due to the cold soil slowing the nematode activity. The maturity and size of some of the leatherjacket larvae also makes passage into the leatherjackets more difficult for nematodes than it would be for entry into the smaller, younger leatherjackets present in lawns later in the summer. If a spring application is to be tried, *Steinernema feltiae*, which can be active at lower temperatures, should be used. The kill rate for spring applications can, though, be minimal.

The optimum time for leatherjacket nematode application is from late August to October. This is when the larvae are still small and the soil warm, which assists the nematodes in two ways: firstly, the warmer soil will mean that the nematodes are more active and more likely to find the leatherjackets; and, secondly, the smaller leatherjackets are more prone to infection and entry by the nematodes.

Leatherjacket lawn damage can be widespread and leatherjackets attract birds to feed on them, causing further damage. KOPPERT BIOLOGICAL SYSTEMS

The required number of applications of leather-jacket-control nematodes will vary, as with chafer grubs, according to the size of the population. Large infestations may require more than one application and it is good practice to apply nematodes twice, with an interval of two weeks. As with chafer-control nem-atodes, for larger areas it is easier to apply with hose-end feeder type applicators or spraying equip-ment with bowsers.

Ants

Ants are more of a nuisance pest on lawns than a par-ticularly damaging one. In some cases, however, ant mounds in high numbers on lawns can start to be a problem. This is a difficult pest to eradicate, as they have few natural enemies that we can harness to con-trol them. Some biological control suppliers offer nematodes as a solution, but I am not yet convinced that they do provide a lasting solution. The strategy is that the nematodes are watered into the ant colonies to disrupt and kill them. In my experience, however, they do not appear to kill many ants. There is perhaps a disruptive influence, which can affect the ant behav-iour, as the application of water and nematodes into the ant mounds may cause them to vacate the colony for a period of a time, but this may not prove worth the investment.

A healthy lawn with a vigorous root system can often prove more resistant to the damage from many turf pests, including chafer grubs and leatherjackets. Chapter 11 on biostimulants will provide some infor-mation on how to achieve this. For successful control of lawn turf pests, the key is careful application of nematodes at the right time and in the correct conditions.

CHAPTER 9

ORNAMENTAL PLANT PESTS AND THEIR NATURAL ENEMIES

There are many insect pests of ornamental plants; too many, in fact, to cover in just this book. This chapter will focus on some of the more commonly occurring pests of ornamental plants and the new insect pest threats.

Vine Weevils

Each year, the Royal Horticultural Society publishes the 'Top 10 Insect Pests', duly nominated by their members. In the majority of years, the vine weevil is placed at either number one or number two on the list. The destruction this insect causes can affect many different ornamental plants. The most common species in the UK is the black vine weevil, *Otiorhynchus sulcatus*. It is a difficult pest to control with insecticides, as it is resistant to many of them, and the adult beetles are difficult to locate. There are also very few insecticides left available for gardeners to use. So why is this insect pest such a problem? To understand this, one needs first to look at the life cycle of the insect.

Vine Weevil Life Cycle

The vine weevil life cycle consists of egg, larva, pupa and adult. Almost all of the adults are female, with a lifespan of between five to twelve months and sometimes even longer. Each female can lay up to 1,000 eggs in this period. These eggs develop into larvae that can survive long periods outdoors, sometimes for as long as nine months. The life cycle is much shorter if the larvae are situated in glasshouses due to the continually warm temperatures. Outdoors, the larvae will stop feeding when the temperatures drop, but indoors, with higher temperatures, they can continue to feed.

Larvae will generally start to pupate and develop into adult beetles during late May and June. The adults are nocturnal and hide throughout the day. They are not winged, but are highly mobile, laying eggs in quite a random pattern. Eggs are laid between July and October and the eggs will hatch into C-shaped larvae with brown heads. The larvae are the most damaging stage of the life cycle for plants.

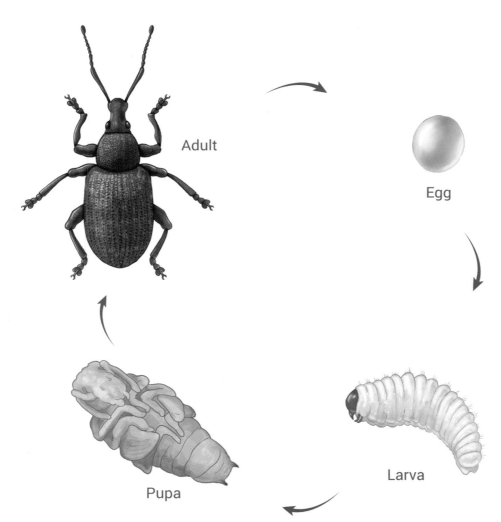

Vine weevil life cycle – how vine weevil develop.
KOPPERT BIOLOGICAL SYSTEMS

Vine Weevil Damage

The larvae of vine weevils will feed on the roots of plants and can destroy root systems, which will lead to eventual plant death. The larvae can even attack the base of a plant. The more mature the vine weevil larvae, the larger the roots they can eat and attack. Many different plant species are attacked, including shrubs, pot plants and fruit-bearing plants. Plants under attack will often wilt. The adult beetles feed on buds and leaves. This damage is quite distinctive, showing as half-moon cuts on the edges of leaves. This feeding does not generally cause significant damage to plants other than in a cosmetic way. It does, however, provide an early warning of the presence of vine weevil in the area.

Biological Control of Vine Weevil

Larvae of beetles, such as vine weevil and chafer grub, can be treated with the nematode *Heterorhabditis bacteriophora*. Nematode treatments are watered into the compost or soil where the larvae are present. This species of nematode searches for the vine weevil grubs in the soil or compost by detecting chemical compounds given off by the larvae. Once located, the nematodes will enter the larvae, releasing a bacterium that kill the larvae within forty-eight hours.

Vine weevil adult – adult vine weevils are nocturnal. SASIMOTO/SHUTTERSTOCK.COM

Vine weevil larvae infected with nematodes (left) compared with uninfected larvae (right). ICL.COM

The infected larvae will eventually turn a red colour. It is also possible to use the nematode species *Steinernema* against vine weevil larvae. This species is more tolerant of the cold and should be used in the spring or late autumn.

When to Apply Vine Weevil Control Nematodes

For outdoor applications, nematode applications can be made from March to May, and again from August to October. The nematodes should be watered into the compost or soil, either by watering can or a hose-end nematode applicator. For indoor infestations, if larvae are found in pots or containers, applications can be made at any time of year.

If applications of nematodes are made at the correct times, they are very effective at controlling vine weevil larvae, especially in pots and containers. New adult vine weevils may appear in gardens each year, migrating in from hedgerows and neighbouring gardens, so repeat applications of nematodes may be required each year. Vine weevil larvae can also be introduced into gardens if they are already present on newly purchases plants, so try to check for signs before purchasing.

There is research under way seeking to develop adult vine weevil traps that will catch the adults using attractants. Hopefully these will become available to gardeners soon. There are also fungi-based products, which can be used against vine weevil larvae, but it is unlikely that these will become available to hobby gardeners.

Box Tree Moth Caterpillars

A relatively new insect pest is the box tree moth (*Cydalima perspectalis*). This is an invasive species that has arrived in Europe and the UK. The caterpillars of this moth are very damaging to the leaves and bark of box trees and plants. Their feeding causes the box plants to dry out and die. Leaves can look skeletal, or may have lots of webbing on them if infected. The box tree caterpillar also absorbs toxic compounds from the box tree leaves when feeding, which makes the caterpillars less attractive to eat to some predators and causes even more of a challenge when seeking to identify natural enemies to apply to control this pest.

Box Tree Moth Life Cycle

The moths lay pale yellow flat eggs, which hatch into greenish-yellow caterpillars with black heads. Mature caterpillars have a green body with dark brown stripes.

Box tree moth – a new invasive species to the UK. EILEEN KUMPF/ SHUTTERSTOCK.COM

Box tree moth caterpillars can be killed with nematodes. ZERBOR/SHUTTERSTOCK.COM

Box tree caterpillar damage – caterpillars can kill box plants.

The adult moth is white with a brown tint to its wings. The time in which the development of the life cycle transpires depends greatly on temperatures. There can be two to three generations of the moth in a year. In a mild winter, some caterpillars will overwinter deep inside the box hedge and start feeding again when temperatures begin to rise.

How to Establish a Programme for Monitoring and Control

The first step in setting up a preventative programme is to detect the presence of box tree caterpillar moths. This will provide advance warning of impending caterpillar infestations. The best way to do this is through the use of box tree moth pheromone traps, which contain sex pheromones to attract the male box tree moths into them. Place the traps next to hedges or box trees, but do not use too many traps, as this can negate the effect of the lures. Depending on weather patterns, this moth could be flying as early as April. Once male moths start to be caught, it can be assumed that mating is taking place and egg laying will follow.

There are some tiny egg parasites sold in France for control of box tree moth eggs, but this species is not native to the UK, so to date is not available to UK gardeners. The natural bacterium, *Bacillus thuringiensis*, which is used by professional growers, is also not permitted for use by hobby gardeners. So, we find ourselves looking at using nematodes against the caterpillars of box tree moths.

How to Use Nematodes against Box Tree Caterpillars

The species of nematode most suited for this task is the *Steinernema carpocapsae*. The key to success when applying nematodes against box tree caterpillars is attempting to get the nematodes into direct contact with the caterpillars. This is sometimes not an easy task, as the caterpillars can be situated quite deep inside the foliage. The best method of application is using a sprayer with a lance, which can get into or close to the foliage. Hose-end nematode applicators can also be used, but be careful that the flow of the water does not wash the nematodes off the caterpillars.

Like other applications of nematodes to leaves and above ground, the conditions should be moist, damp and overcast. This gives the nematodes the best chance of surviving long enough on the leaves to infect and get inside the caterpillars, where they will release a bacterium to kill the caterpillars. In many cases, more than one application will be required to kill large numbers of the caterpillars. Weekly applications should be applied until the caterpillar numbers decline.

Horse-Chestnut Leaf Miners

Another invasive pest that has arrived in the UK and has established over much of the country is the horse-chestnut leaf miner moth (*Cameraria ohridella*). This tiny moth attacks horse-chestnut tree leaves. The larvae of the moth bore into the leaves, establishing white leaf mines all over them. Eventually the leaves go brown and die, causing early leaf fall. This does not kill the trees, but weakens them and makes them more prone to diseases.

How to Protect Horse-Chestnut Trees

Not much research has been conducted into discovering treatments against this new pest, most likely because horse-chestnut trees are not as commercially significant as other plants. There are some steps that can be taken to reduce the damage, however. The leaf miner moths pupate in the old leaves at the base of the tree. If they are left there, they will emerge the following spring to lay more eggs and cause further damage. A simple way to reduce this is to remove and burn the old leaves.

It is also possible to use horse-chestnut leaf miner pheromone traps to catch the male moths. Unlike some pheromone traps, these traps can catch very high numbers of horse-chestnut leaf miner moths. They do not catch enough to stop the damage, but it can be satisfying to catch so many moths in a trap and it will help to reduce the overall population.

Natural Enemies of the Horse-Chestnut Leaf Miner

There are so far no commercially available natural enemies for this pest, but nature is starting to lend a helping hand. Populations of blue tit birds enjoy feeding on the moths and can be observed in the trees

Horse-chestnut leaf miner adult – tiny moths that hatch in large numbers. RADU BERCAN/ SHUTTERSTOCK.COM

Horse-chestnut leaf miner leaf damage. The leaves eventually go brown and drop early.

doing just that. Attempting to encourage the presence of such birds with nesting boxes could prove a worthwhile strategy.

Red Lily Beetles

This is another infamous insect that appears regularly in gardeners' surveys of troublesome new pests. The red lily beetle (*Lilioceris lilii*) is a damaging pest of lily and fritillaria plants. The adult beetles are red and generally quite an attractive beetle, but do not be taken in by this! They will feed on leaves, making holes, and the larvae are capable of eating all of a plant's leaves. This destroys the appearance of the plant and can lead to the formation of smaller bulbs than usual.

The red lily beetle is included in this book, not as an example of a pest with natural enemies that can be deployed against it, but rather as an example of how sometimes nature can be clever in finding ways of protecting itself against attack. The adult beetles cover their larvae in frass to prevent predators eating them, which proves to be very effective.

How to Protect Plants from the Lily Beetle

The adult lily beetles overwinter in the soil, not always where the bulbs are. Birds and predatory beetles, like rove beetles, may feed on them, so disturbing the soil may help. Manual removal of the adults whenever they are observed and cleaning the leaves of the larvae will also help. Also look out for plant breeds claiming resistance to this pest. Another interesting research area concerns whether the plant can be made less attractive to such a pest with the addition of a biostimulant and nutrients such as calcium, and this will be explored more in the next chapter.

Viburnum Beetles

Viburnum shrubs and plants are often attacked by the viburnum beetle, *Pyrrhalta viburni*. Leaves can become discoloured and may have brown edging, or they may be shredded by the larvae of these beetles. The larvae are a grey to brown colour. The beetle stage of the

Red lily beetle – a harmless looking beetle, but an unwelcome sight on lily plants. SERHII SHCHERBYNA/ SHUTTERSTOCK.COM

Viburnum beetle larvae will shred leaves, but can be treated with nematodes.

viburnum beetle life cycle will lay eggs that overwinter on the host plants. For many years, the only solution was the manual removal of the larvae, or the use of insecticides.

New Nematode Control for Viburnum Larvae

The larvae of the viburnum beetle appear on viburnums from April to about mid-June in the UK. This provides a window of opportunity to apply nematodes to the larvae. The nematode frequently used against other leaf- and stem-dwelling pests can also be used (*Steinernema carpocapsae*) against viburnum beetle larvae. As with other above-ground applications of nematodes, the key to success is to ensure that the nematodes come directly into contact with the larvae on the leaf and in the right conditions. It is important to choose a warm, damp, humid day and to avoid applying the nematodes in bright sunshine. This latest use of nematodes provides another great alternative to chemical solutions.

Ornamental plant pests occur over a huge variety of plants and not all pests will have natural enemies that can be introduced by the gardener against them. This is often because the research has not been completed into solutions for what may be viewed as minor, or less commercially impactful, insect pests. Research is often only instigated when plants have a commercial value, that is, they are used for producing food, or are sold in large numbers as ornamental plants. This is where knowledge from sites such as botanical gardens becomes invaluable, as they generally look after and maintain very diverse plant collections. Botanical gardens are often implementing and applying the use of natural enemies on many different plant species. Their results and findings often lead to knowledge that can be passed on to gardeners. Gardeners can then implement these new ways of using natural enemies against different plant pests. Nature also finds ways of helping, such as when blue tit bird populations start feeding on new pests like the horse-chestnut leaf miner. The challenge to find natural solutions for ornamental plant pests, though, is likely to be a continual one.

CHAPTER 10

BIOLOGICAL CONTROL AND NATURAL ENEMIES IN ACTION AT BOTANICAL GARDENS

Botanical gardens and gardens run by institutions such as the Royal Horticultural Society (RHS) and the National Trust are now becoming pioneers in the use of natural enemies and biological control. Many of these sites look after huge numbers of different plant species and have set climates specially designed to provide the natural habitat for such plants. These climates can also, unfortunately, provide the ideal environment for the insect pests of these plants, but it is encouraging to note that the sites are recognizing the role that natural enemies can play in controlling these pests. In this chapter, we will look at why the professional gardeners at these sites are opting to use biological control and how they do so.

Why are Public Gardens using Biological Control?

The primary explanation for the switch to biological control is purely the desire and aim of leading botanical and public gardens to reduce or eliminate pesticide use on their sites. I asked David Knott, the curator of living collections at the Royal Botanic Garden Edinburgh (RBGE), for his opinion on biological control being used at his site:

> The benefits of using biological control at the Royal Botanic Garden Edinburgh have been both obvious and on occasion surprising. Key has been staff monitoring the plants in their care and also understanding the pest and the biological control required. The obvious benefits have been their effectiveness in controlling pests and removing the need for staff to apply pesticides, which in turn has created a more pleasant working environment. This pesticide-free environment has also created a considerably better visitor experience, prompting comments from visitors that the fragrances and scents in the glasshouses reminded them of their childhood or their holidays!

The increased use of biological control at professional gardens has also been driven by a range of other factors, which have all contributed to an overwhelming

Royal Botanic Garden Edinburgh Palm House, one of the most historic and impressive glasshouses in the UK.

conviction among gardeners that the application of pesticides should no longer be viewed as a viable form of pest control on their sites. Health is one such factor; professional gardeners simply do not want to work with potentially toxic insecticides. Not only are they concerned about the health risks of working with such products, but they also dislike having to follow strict guidelines in the application of the chemicals. Such guidelines include having to wear uncomfortable and bulky protective clothing, which is not a pleasant experience when working inside hot greenhouses. Gardeners must also ensure that they shut down and cordon off areas where they are applying these pesticides in order to protect the general public from any exposure to potentially toxic chemicals. These areas may have to remain closed at times when visitors wish to view the plant collections that are being treated, which can impact the overall enjoyment that visitors have during their visits.

It is not only the health of humans that can be at risk when pesticides are applied, but also the plants themselves and indeed any beneficial insects that are located near the treated plants. Repeated applications of insecticides can stunt or slow plant growth and, if applied in hot conditions, can sometimes scorch and damage the plants. Pollinating insects, such as bees or adult lacewings, may be directly harmed or killed following the application of insecticides. The reduction of pollinators in specific garden areas can have a big impact on the viability of plant collections and the ability of such plants to produce seeds. Nature provides plenty of naturally occurring predators and parasites of insect pests, such as ladybirds and hoverfly larvae for aphid control. An application of an insecticide to kill one pest may cause an explosion in population growth of another pest species by killing the natural enemies of this other pest.

Professional gardeners also know by experience that the success of insecticide applications will decline over time, especially with repeated use. Insect pests become resistant to synthetic insecticides the more they are used, just as humans may become less resistant to certain illnesses if the same antibiotics are overused. Professional gardeners, like hobby gardeners, also have a decreasing armoury of insecticides to choose from and find it difficult to rotate different chemicals to counter this problem. The result of this is that the remaining insecticides inevitably become less effective over time and fail to provide a solution to the insect pests prevalent on sites open to the public. The use of biological control and the natural enemies of pests, however, now provide a better solution, as insects cannot become resistant to their natural enemies.

Botanical and Public Gardens Helping to Improve New Biological Control Methods for Garden Pests

Some of the leading gardens in the UK are playing a crucial role in helping to find new biological control solutions for garden insect pests. This is partly because

much of the conducted research into new pest solutions has been based on insect pests that attack commercial crops. There has been very little research dedicated to the pests that occur in gardens, and the knowledge and experience that has been formulated is not always readily available. Professional gardens therefore often must find, and test, new ways of using existing natural enemies against new or rarer insect pests.

Another reason that public gardens are having to find new biological control methods is because the number of different plant species held in their collections may have many different pests, whereas in commercial crops there are normally only one or two major pests. This can represent an even bigger research challenge for the public gardens, but such situations do often mirror what can happen in private plant collections or normal gardens, so the research findings can be of great benefit to hobby gardeners. They can visit professional gardens to learn how biological control is being used and then apply many of

Biological control products being put out at Cambridge University Botanic Garden.

the same principles and techniques to their own gardens. The use of natural enemies can sometimes be quite visible in botanical and other gardens.

In the past, curators of public gardens may have wished to hide evidence from the public that they were taking steps to control pests, as they may have wished to pretend such gardens had no pests at all! They may also have been concerned about directing interest away from their fantastic plant collections, but this mindset is changing. The use of natural pest control methods is now popular and appreciated by most garden visitors, who, in many cases, are very interested in the process and wish to learn more. Education has a big role to play in the successful adoption of biological control by gardeners and professional gardens can further enhance their great reputations by educating visitors on the use of natural enemies as an alternative, and better, solution to insect pest problems, rather than insecticide use.

For the rest of this chapter, we will look at some case studies regarding biological control methods from leading professional gardens in the UK.

Case Study 1: Mealybugs and Cockroaches

The RBGE and Cambridge University Botanic Garden (CUBG) both house some fantastic plant collections, many of which are unique and of national importance to Scotland, England and the world. Some of these collections have been maintained for years and have an amazing history; a visit to either site is always fascinating and well worthwhile.

One of the challenges in maintaining historical and exotic plant collections is insect pest control. Some plants in these collections are not native to the UK and require very precise climate conditions and particular care to maintain their health. Some of the plants in these collections are also very large and mature, which provides the opportunity for insect pests to hide and breed on them without gardeners necessarily being able to access them easily to apply control measures. These conditions can provide the ideal environment for multiple insect pests to develop.

Once a certain pest becomes established in one of these complex micro-environments, its numbers may not only become difficult to control, but it can also be difficult to prevent the pests from becoming very noticeable. Some of these pests will damage plants and leave visible evidence of their presence. One such pest is the mealybug. This pest can also occur on houseplants and greenhouses, where they can cause serious damage. Learning how to control this pest using one of its natural enemies is very valuable to both the professional and the hobby gardener.

Some botanical gardens, such as the RBGE and CUBG, have been using biological control, in the form of the predatory beetle *Cryptolaemus montrouzieri*, against the mealybug for many years, but with limited success. Mealybug populations were still very visible to visitors, as was the secondary damage caused by the mealybugs leaving sticky honeydew on plants, which led to the growth of large areas of black mould. This was very unattractive for visitors and was impairing plant health in collections. So why, with the *Cryptolaemus* predator beetles having been applied and introduced in near perfect conditions for them to thrive, were they failing to control the mealybug?

The answer was not a straightforward one and in fact several factors were preventing this biological control from working as effectively as it should have done. Both sites were committed to finding a solution and the first step was to eliminate any practices or conditions that would prevent the *Cryptolaemus* beetles from establishing on the collections.

Ditch the Clean-Up Spray

One of the practices many horticulturalists adopt is to clear up in the autumn. Old plant growth is removed and sometimes 'clean-up' pesticides are applied to kill insect pests before the winter, so as to prevent them from overwintering and causing problems the following spring. This practice, however, was impacting the survival and establishment of the *Cryptolaemus* predators. The climate in the glasshouses, even in the winter, can provide conditions suitable for the *Cryptolaemus* to survive. Unfortunately, the application of clean-up insecticides killed off any *Cryptolaemus* predators that might have made it through the winter. This meant that new populations had to be established each spring and summer. The clean-up sprays were also ineffective in killing many mealybugs, as these are difficult to kill with insecticide sprays. Both sites thankfully stopped using the clean-up sprays, which allowed

Cryptolaemus larvae feeding and eating mealybugs.
PROTASOV AN/SHUTTERSTOCK.COM

bigger populations of the predatory beetles to survive and breed again to combat the mealybugs in the spring and summer.

Numbers Game and Larvae

The traditional approach for many sites using *Cryptolaemus* was to introduce small amounts of the adult beetles in greenhouses throughout the spring and summer, the idea being that the winged adults would locate any mealybug infestations and keep their numbers in check. This did not always work, however, with large populations of mealybugs establishing on certain plant types with few or no predators present to control their numbers. It could have been that the adult *Cryptolaemus* naturally migrated to the light and headed towards plant tops near vents and windows, leaving many plants lower down without a predator presence. It is difficult to apply winged predators in one specific area, so targeting a particular infestation on one, or several, plants could be problematic. Mealybugs can also produce large populations,

especially in warmer conditions, so a small number of predatory beetles introduced every few weeks was not enough to contain and control large populations of the mealybug.

The answer at RBGE and CUBG was to introduce large numbers of the larval stage of the *Cryptolaemus* beetle. The larvae were introduced and placed directly on to the most heavily infested plants in unit sizes of 1,000 *Cryptolaemus* larvae. They were then precisely where they needed to be and began feeding on the mealybug immediately. Although not winged, the larvae are mobile and will travel over the plants, seeking and consuming high numbers of mealybugs and their eggs. For inaccessible and difficult to reach locations, the larvae were poured into small distribution boxes with hooks that were hung on to the plants. The larvae then proceeded to exit the boxes and locate the mealybugs.

This process was repeated two to three times in the spring and summer, with much higher numbers of predators being released than in the previous years. The initial cost was much higher than the introduction

Distribution boxes on cycad plants at Cambridge University Botanic Garden to help distribute *Cryptolaemus* larvae.

of low numbers of predatory beetles, but the results soon started to pay off. The rapid build-up of predatory larvae had a significant impact on the mealybug populations. Plants that had been hosting huge numbers of mealybugs, such as the cycads, became infested with significantly fewer mealybugs and over a few years, whole greenhouses started to be rid of the pest. *Cryptolaemus* levels started to maintain themselves in certain areas, aided by the fact that clean-up sprays were no longer used and killing them in the winter. Subsequent introductions of large numbers of predatory larvae were then no longer required, which reduced the costs.

Whilst the mealybug population has not been eradicated entirely on either site, the numbers are now much more manageable and the damage to plants significantly reduced. This system has also helped to create a better ecosystem within the glasshouses, where low numbers of mealybug can be tolerated, as the greenhouses also contain healthy populations of one their natural predators, the *Cryptolaemus*.

Mealybug Control Strategy Continues to Evolve

Other natural enemies have been deployed at RBGE and CUBG to assist the *Cryptolaemus*. This is partly due to the fact that the effectiveness of successful predators, such as the *Cryptolaemus*, can still be limited when the environmental conditions do not quite provide the conditions required for them to reproduce or be highly active. This may be when there is limited daylight, or when temperatures are lower, for instance. Both sites are now therefore starting to introduce tiny parasitic wasps against the mealybugs to supplement and enhance the biological control over this pest. These parasites are very specific and will only attack mealybugs. The advantage of using these wasps, over the *Cryptolaemus*, is that they can be deployed at slightly lower temperatures and do not require lots of sunshine hours to reproduce.

One such wasp species is the citrus mealybug parasite: *Anagyrus pseudococci*. This tiny wasp injects

Parasitic wasp attacking a mealybug. KOPPERT BIOLOGICAL SYSTEMS

Mealybug parasite exit hole. KOPPERT BIOLOGICAL SYSTEMS

The impressive Palm House interior at Royal Botanic Garden Edinburgh.

its egg into the mealybug adult, where the egg develops inside the mealybug and the hatched wasp larva kills the mealybug before emerging from its body. These parasites are highly mobile inside the glasshouses, flying around and detecting mealybugs to parasitize. The presence of the parasites can help to control early mealybug infestations and can be used in combination with the *Cryptolaemus* predators.

One area in which it has been difficult to reduce chemical pesticides is in the control of cockroaches. The warm, humid conditions of tropical greenhouses can provide an ideal breeding site for cockroaches, especially under the floor slabs, and some species will feed on vegetation and cause damage. Cockroaches also pose a threat to human health as they can spread disease and infections. Until very recently, the only control method available for treating cockroach infestations was to use insecticides and, for sites attempting to move away from the use of pesticides, this was a frustrating exception.

In Scotland, a release licence has been granted to use a new cockroach parasite, the *Aprostocetus hagenowii*. This can be released against cockroaches that produce egg sacs, where the tiny parasitic wasp will lay its eggs inside the cockroach eggs, which then hatch and prevent the cockroach eggs from developing. The RBGE will shortly implement the new parasite into its insect pest control programme to further the aim of creating pesticide-free gardens. Glasgow Botanic Gardens has also started testing these newly available parasites. These instances represent another exciting example of how the use of natural enemies is expanding into new areas and for the treatment of different insect pests.

Case Study 2: Multiple Challenges of Insect Pest Control at a Show Garden

The Royal Horticultural Society Garden Hyde Hall in Essex showcases the best in British gardening and garden design. It provides inspiration to visitors and educates gardeners on the best practices in gardening. Like the botanical gardens, the Royal Horticultural Society (RHS) also wishes to move away from the use of pesticides. The site at Hyde Hall covers a large area incorporating different planting schemes, a production nursery and the unique global glasshouse.

A floral display Royal Horticultural Society Garden Hyde Hall.

RHS Hyde Hall nursery glasshouse, where biological control is used all year round to control insect pests.

These varied environments throw up different challenges for insect pest control and this case study shows how biological control and the use of natural enemies play a key role in keeping pest levels at a minimum.

Start Clean

Many of the plants at Hyde Hall start their life at the site production nursery. This glasshouse area can host many different plant species and as such has the potential to attract a variety of pests. The glasshouse is also home to a lot of propagation activity, with cuttings and seedlings grown to produce plants for the main site. It is therefore very important to control insect pests from the start to enable these plants to have a healthy start and to ensure that only the vigorous, strong and healthy plants will leave the nursery, or are kept on at the nursery as stock plants.

Sciarid Flies

One of the most significant insect pests that threatens young plants is the larvae of the sciarid fly. These tiny flies will build up in warm and moist conditions. The adult flies like to lay their eggs in seed trays and in pots of compost, which then develop into tiny white larvae. These larvae then feed on seedling and cuttings roots, and in severe cases cause these plants to collapse and die. At the Hyde Hall nursery this danger is negated with the use of nematodes, where, during the propagation period, regular applications of nematodes are watered into the seed trays and pots. The nematodes will then seek out and kill the larvae. General adult sciarid fly populations are monitored by counting the number of adult flies caught on yellow sticky traps. If there is a pattern of increasing fly activity, extra nematode applications are applied, which quickly kill off any developing sciarid fly larvae.

Sciarid fly larvae in compost can be controlled with nematodes. KOPPERT BIOLOGICAL SYSTEMS

To supplement the nematodes, a predatory mite is also applied to pots and compost a couple of times a year. The *Macrocheles robustulus* is different to most other predatory mites in that it is active on and within the compost. It feeds on any small larvae it finds there, including the sciarid fly larvae. This mite offers a useful additional background control for these pests and other small pest larvae and pupae that may occur in the compost.

Assorted Pests

A preventative control programme of natural enemies is also introduced to the main glasshouse area to suppress pests throughout the spring and summer. This includes the regular introductions of aphid parasites, which patrol the glass pursuing any aphids that may have snuck into the structure.

If large colonies of aphids do appear, a combined programme of predator introductions is then rolled out to consume the aphids. This includes lacewing larvae and a midge! The gall midge, *Aphidoletes aphidimyza*, is introduced as a pupa in a bottle, from which it hatches and flies to the aphid colonies, laying its eggs amongst them. These eggs then develop into tiny orange larvae, which consume huge quantities of aphids.

Aphid parasite in action. KOPPERT BIOLOGICAL SYSTEMS

Other pests, such as spider mites and thrips, are also likely to appear in a glasshouse full of so many different plants. In order to prevent these pests from establishing, a programme of predatory mites is released, consisting of specific predators to spider mites and thrips. These predators are supplied in sachets that are hung on plants and I will elaborate on this method when I cover the Global House introduction programme.

Parasites in action at RHS
Hyde Hall Garden.

Aphidoletes larvae feeding on
aphids, which they consume in
large numbers. KOPPERT
BIOLOGICAL SYSTEMS

Emerging Pest

A pest that is becoming generally more prevalent under glass is the tortrix moth. There are several species of these moths, but the most commonly occurring one under glass is called the carnation tortrix moth. This moth lays eggs on a wide range of plants, but often on shrubs. The eggs develop into caterpillars that feed on leaves and defoliate plants. The caterpillars will wrap themselves in leaves, making it difficult to reach and treat them. Early infestations can be physically picked off, but caterpillars can be missed, especially at busy visitor times at these sites.

In response to this issue, Hyde Hall, in the nursery glasshouse area, has opted to use a tiny egg parasite called the *Trichogramma evanescens*. This wasp has been introduced to kill and parasitize the moth eggs. The wasps are supplied as eggs in a card, from which they hatch and fly off to locate the moth eggs. The use of this parasitic wasp against the carnation tortrix moth is quite a recent innovation, but early signs indicate that regular introductions of the parasites will reduce the tortrix moth numbers quite significantly.

The Global House

The Global House at Hyde Hall grows edible produce, with the aim of growing such produce all year round. This is a challenge with the different weather seasons in the UK, but a challenge that is being met. Hyde Hall is using alternative plant cultivars and new techniques to grow plants outside of their traditional growing period. These conditions also, however, often provide the environment for insect pests of these crops to establish. More than ever, a chemical-free method of insect pest control is required when dealing with edible crops and plants, especially in a venue with as many visitors as the Global House attracts.

In the summer months, when the Global House is full of cucumbers, peppers, aubergines and sometimes rather unusual salads that are being tested, the potential for an insect pest invasion can be quite high. The main pest threats are from spider mites and especially from aphids.

Aphid Control Programme

One of the advantages of a pesticide-free glasshouse in the summer is the number of natural aphid predators that can arrive once aphids appear on the plants. This includes different species of ladybirds, including their larvae and adult stages, which both feed on aphids. Other aphid predators will also appear, such as hoverfly larvae and naturally occurring gall midge larvae. These predators all contribute to keeping the aphid population in check. The only problem is that sometimes they arrive too late in the summer, when large numbers of aphids may already be feeding on the plants.

For this reason, a programme of aphid natural enemies can be introduced from the start of the season to protect the crops and plants before aphid populations establish. The main biological control defence is provided in the form of a bottle of aphid parasites called Aphiscout. Aphiscout contains five different aphid parasites, covering all of the common species of aphid present in the UK. This ensures that any aphid species entering the glasshouse can be controlled with parasitization. The parasites are introduced every two weeks in the spring and summer to ensure a constant predator presence in the Global House. Even with this line of defence, however, aphid pressure can be high

The Global House at RHS Hyde Hall Garden.

Hoverfly larvae eat aphids and often occur naturally when no pesticides have been applied.
MUDDY KNEES/SHUTTERSTOCK.COM

and plants such as aubergines, for example, attract very high numbers of aphids.

The normal treatment pattern that occurs is that very high levels of aphid parasites and aphid mummies will appear on the plants, which prevents serious damage to the plants, but can sometimes still leave quite high numbers of aphids present. This is not all bad though, as this is the time when the natural population of aphid predators from outside the glasshouse are attracted in to feed on the aphids. As with the mealybug control, referred to earlier in the chapter, this is when a positive ecosystem of pest and natural enemy will develop to deny the pests the ability to cause serious damage, yet still leave enough pests present to harbour a healthy population of the natural enemies.

Other pests that can be encountered in the Global House include the two-spotted spider mite and thrips, both of which have the potential to damage plants and reduce yields. A programme of predatory mite introductions against spider mite and thrips, however, has been largely successful in preventing these pests from causing much damage. Small, slow-release sachets of predators are hung on the plants, releasing predators to patrol the plants for several weeks. This treatment has prevented harmful levels of spider mite and thrips from establishing.

Moving away from the Global House, we now head outside into the gardens to encounter a relatively new non-native pest in the UK.

Strategy to Control Box Tree Moth

Box tree moths and their caterpillars are a new insect pest at Hyde Hall, as they are for much of England. This non-native insect pest is rapidly spreading up England from the south-east. For a garden open to the public, this moth causes some very unsightly damage to box hedges, with large areas becoming defoliated. The curator at RHS Hyde Hall, Mr Robert Brett, therefore wished to find a natural solution, which visitors could also use in their gardens.

The first step was to use box tree moth pheromone traps to monitor when the moths were active and to help reduce the male moth population, which in turn would lead to less mating and less egg laying. This is not a control method, but part of a strategy to reduce population numbers.

In another area, a new pheromone disruptor system was deployed. This is when a high concentration of pheromones is applied to plants to confuse box tree moths and ultimately prevent them breeding. The early results were positive, but more work needs to be done with this technique and it is not yet clear whether

The box tree pheromone trap trial at RHS Hyde Hall Garden.

these products will be available for hobby gardeners to utilize just yet.

Nematodes Against Box Tree Caterpillars

Nematodes used for insect pest control are accessible to gardeners and are relatively easy to apply. Hyde Hall has been spraying them directly on to box tree caterpillars identified in the garden's box hedges. This can be quite difficult, however, as the nematodes must be sprayed directly on to the caterpillars, which can be located inside the hedge. To reach their targets, the gardeners at Hyde Hall had to use knapsack sprayers with lances attached to ensure that the nematode solution came into contact with the box tree caterpillars. The results were difficult to ascertain, as quite severe damage still occurred in many areas, but the hedges treated with nematodes generally had less damage than the hedges not treated. The lesson to be learnt here is that more applications of nematodes were required, as the population kill was not enough to prevent damage to the box plants. Generally, for severe infestations of pests, repeat applications of nematodes are often required to bring population numbers down.

This is still a very new way of using nematodes, however, and especially against a formidable pest that can survive in quite harsh conditions. As with many new biological controls tried by professional gardeners, like those at the RHS, techniques need refining and more needs to be known about both the pests and the relevant natural enemies to be used against them.

Case Study 3: New Biological Control Strategy for Thrip Control at the National Botanic Garden of Wales

Some insect pests become more prevalent over time. This can be for several reasons, such as global warming, which is leading to milder winters and warmer summers. This aids the ability of insect pests to reproduce and establish in higher numbers. Another potential reason for renewed insect pest growth may be because non-discriminate insecticides applied in the past suppressed some insect pests, especially

The National Botanic Garden of Wales, which is looking at new ways of applying biological control, including the use of drones.

when used in greenhouses, but are now no longer being applied. One pest that may have benefitted from such changes to conditions is the glasshouse/greenhouse thrip, (*Heliothrips haemorrhoidalis*). This thrip species was not thought of as a problem for glasshouse-cultivated plants until quite recently, when its numbers have risen rapidly.

The most common thrip species to cause a problem to glasshouse-grown plants is the western flower thrip (*Frankliniella occidentalis*). This species attacks many plants and glasshouse-grown crops, so for this reason it has had quite a lot of research dedicated to it in order to discover the necessary effective natural enemies. Unfortunately, it appears that most of these natural enemies do not like to feed on glasshouse thrip larvae. This may be because the larvae are larger and the predatory mites used against western flower thrip feed on the small thrip larvae. Another control measure and monitoring system available for western flower thrip infestations is the use of sticky insect traps. Again, unfortunately, glasshouse thrip adults do

not fly as much as western flower thrips, so it has been difficult to catch them on the traps.

Damage Symptoms

The damage that glasshouse thrips cause can be significant to a wide range of plants. They can devastate large areas of plants by feeding on the leaves, with damage symptoms including leaves turning a silvery colour, before they are eventually killed by the thrip. Although the adults are not as mobile as some thrip species, the glasshouse thrip can spread over large areas of plants. The thrips also deposit black frass droplets on the leaves, which makes infected plants even more unsightly.

The adult thrip is black, very small and pencil-shaped, with yellow-green larvae. Both the larvae and the adults will be visible on leaves. This thrip species can also appear outside on shrubs before moving inside. In some situations, their rate of spread across plants appeared to be slow, but in recent years at an increasing number of sites this spread has increased, with more plant varieties showing damage and a greater number of plants becoming infected.

Glasshouse Thrip at the National Botanic Garden of Wales

One of the public gardens to see a steady increase in the damage from this thrip species is the National Botanic Garden of Wales (NBGW). Damage to date has been mostly located in the greenhouses and quite large numbers of thrip are now present on some plants in the impressive Great House, which includes ferns and other shrubs. The management staff and gardeners of NBGW are understandably keen to find a way to control and, if possible, eradicate this pest. The site is committed to reducing and eliminating the use of insecticides, so is looking towards a natural solution to control this increasingly difficult insect pest.

The search for an effective natural enemy, or combination of natural enemies, has begun. Like many pests of ornamental plants there is little reference or literature to draw upon to learn more about how to control this insect pest. A new approach is therefore required, yet this situation provides another positive example of how the UK's leading public gardens are adapting to changes in pest control and are now searching for natural solutions.

Using Existing Natural Enemies in a Different Way

To date, there are so far no specific natural enemies available in the UK to control this thrip species effectively. The first step is therefore to see if a more general insect predator could be used. Is there one in our armoury already that would feed on this pesky thrip? Most of the current thrip predators for western flower thrip feed on the larval stage. Could a larger predator be used to feed on the glasshouse thrip larvae? And what is that predator?

A potential candidate is a predator with a big appetite and a very large pair of jaws – the lacewing larva. These insects are more commonly known for their use in controlling infestations of aphids and greenfly, but if no aphids are present they have been observed feeding on other insects on leaf surfaces, including spider mites and leaf hopper larvae. It is their ability to eat the leaf hopper larvae that gives some hope that they might also feed on glasshouse thrip larvae, which are of similar size and appearance to the leaf hoppers.

Glasshouse thrip damage, a damaging new thrip species.

A trial to test this is, at the time of writing, about to get under way. The idea is to introduce large numbers of lacewing larvae to the leaves of plants infected with glasshouse thrip larvae for several consecutive weeks. By introducing large numbers, the hope is that the thrip larvae will be swamped by the high numbers of predatory larvae. Any other pest in this scenario would quickly be consumed and the lacewing larvae would then only be left with the glasshouse thrip larvae or themselves to eat!

Lacewing adults do not eat other insects, so once the larvae develop into lacewing adults, they are no longer an insect predator, which is another reason why regular applications of their larvae on plants are required to maintain their presence. The life cycle of the larvae is quite a long one and is dependent upon temperatures, plus the larvae are also largely nocturnal, so monitoring their populations in the day can be difficult. Will these voracious lacewing larvae provide a solution? Only time will tell! Sometimes the only way to know is to try and many biological control solutions have been proven in this way.

Other solutions may include the use of natural fungi against thrips. There are products available to professional gardeners for this use, but they are unlikely to become available to hobby gardeners.

Gaining Access to Specific Predators and Parasites

Most insect pests do have a specific natural enemy out there somewhere. There can be numerous problems, however, in sourcing and getting permission to use such natural enemies. Many countries, including the UK, will only permit the use of native natural enemies, unless it can be proven that the non-native insects cannot establish in the UK, or have no negative impacts on the ecology of the country, and few would argue against this logic. There are exceptions, however, for the use of natural enemies in confined and heated environments, such as glasshouses. Sometimes it can be proven that non-native natural enemies can be released in these environments without damage to the ecology outside these structures, especially if they are unable to survive a British winter.

In Northern Europe, which has a climate not dissimilar to the UK, there are some specific predators and parasites produced to combat glasshouse thrip, and applications to the UK government and Welsh government to obtain a release licence for these insects are under way. It is too early to tell whether there is enough data available to support successful applications, but respected institutions like the NBGW are lending their support to these applications, as they may provide yet another pesticide-free solution to a damaging insect pest.

All of the leading gardens and institutions cited in this chapter are working hard and lending their support to finding pesticide-free and natural methods to control insect pests. Much of the work carried out on these sites directly benefits gardeners in the UK and further afield, as new techniques and methods are evaluated which may lead to new natural solutions becoming available.

Clean lily pads at Royal Botanic Garden Edinburgh following the introduction of aphid parasites.

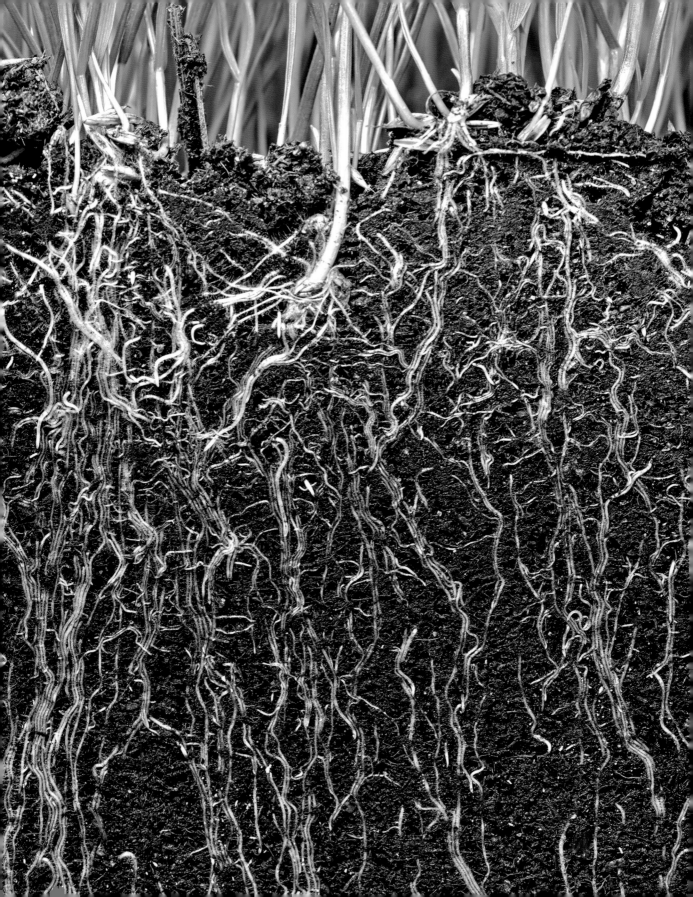

CHAPTER 11

BIOSTIMULANTS

This chapter may appear to be the odd one out in a book primarily concerning the use of natural enemies against insect pests. The development and increased use of biostimulants, however, can have a direct influence on the ability of plants to resist pests and diseases. In this chapter, we will look at what they are and how their increased use can help gardeners.

What are Biostimulants?

A general definition of biostimulants used in horticulture is as follows: 'A plant biostimulant contains substances and/or micro-organisms that stimulate natural plant processes. The effect will be independent of its nutrient content and will improve one or more of

Seaweed is a key ingredient of many biostimulants.

IMAGE OPPOSITE:
DIVEDOG/
SHURTTERSTOCK.COM

the following characteristics of the plant, or the plant rhizosphere.'

Biostimulants are normally made from plant-derived ingredients and microbial elements, such as natural fungi and bacteria. These can be supplied in several different formats. Some will be made of liquid formulations, for instance, which will often include seaweed and plant-based ingredients that are to be diluted and watered into growing media. Other biostimulants can be made up of quite complex granules that incorporate fungi, bacteria and some fertilizer elements, which are to be applied when planting, or as a top dressing to the soil. There are also some soluble powder formulations available that can be mixed with water before being applied.

Professional growers and gardeners who maintain sports turf or large grassland sites increasingly see the value of these products as a means to stimulate natural microbial life in soils, which in turn helps plants and grass to become more resistant to disease and pests. The previous use of synthetic and man-made fertilizers has reduced the natural levels of fungi and bacteria in the soil, which now needs to be built up again. Gardeners can access an increasing number of these products, especially those including mycorrhizal fungi, which are already being widely used.

How Can Biostimulants Help Plants to Fight Pests and Diseases?

Biostimulants can help plants function more efficiently. One of these processes includes the ability to convert amino acids into proteins. When this process goes wrong and there is a build of amino acids in the plants, this often attracts pests such as whitefly and aphids. When plants absorb too much nitrogen or have an imbalance, there is often an increase in pests such as the mealybug. If the absorption and uptake of nutrients and water is carried out efficiently by plants, they become more resilient and less attractive to pests and less prone to plant diseases. Put simply, weak plants attract pests and diseases; strong ones, less so.

Healthy Roots, Healthy Plant

In the previous chapters, I have discussed how important it is to protect plant roots from pests that will eat and ultimately destroy them. Equally as important a factor is to create the conditions to stimulate healthy root growth. The more efficiently plants can absorb water and nutrients, the stronger their growth and health will be. Roots interact all the time with the soil life and micro-organisms around them. Beneficial fungi and bacteria have a very positive effect on the development of these roots, so biostimulants containing them can help to restore soil life. The establishment of a strong root system provides the basis for continued healthy plant growth.

The Benefits of Mycorrhizal Fungi

One of the biostimulants already used by some gardeners is mycorrhizal fungi. These fungi have a symbiotic relationship with the plant. They help the plant roots to take up more moisture and nutrients, whilst providing nutrition for the fungi. Plant roots that have a healthy active mycorrhizal fungi population working with them tend to have a far more developed root system than those that do not have the fungi. There are many different varieties of mycorrhizal fungi and finding out which types benefit which plants can require some serious research! Thankfully, most commercially available mycorrhizal products consist of a mix of different types of fungi, providing a good combination that will benefit the majority of plants.

Roses are one of the groups of plants that seem to benefit especially from the addition of mycorrhizal fungi at planting. Most leading rose producers recommend, and often sell, mycorrhiza-based products to be used when planting their roses. Some gardeners also report that areas of the garden where rose plant disease has been present in the soil can again be planted with roses, if mycorrhizal fungi is also used.

The benefits of mycorrhiza are evidenced much more clearly when used in soils with poor nutrition levels, or in harsh environments for plants, such as building sites or roadsides. Mycorrhizal fungi also help plants to withstand drought and water shortage for longer periods. This is because the fungi are helping plants to extract and absorb as much available moisture

Roses grown with mycorrhizal fungi. NOVOZYMES BIOLOGICAL

and nutrient as possible from the surrounding area. If gardeners have a healthy soil, with plenty of organic content, the benefits of mycorrhiza will be less obvious, as roots and plants should be able to grow in a healthy way unaided.

Trichoderma Fungi

There are other forms of fungi that act as biostimulants, including some strains of *Trichoderma* fungi. These fungi also stimulate increased root growth and can outcompete the space taken up by harmful fungi in the soil. This also helps to prevent the establishment of soil-borne diseases. Some strains of *Trichoderma* are now being developed as biological fungicides for use by professional growers. Unfortunately, these are unlikely to become products available to gardeners in the UK.

Plant-Derived Biostimulants

Seaweed extracts are often incorporated into many varieties of biostimulant products and their benefits are recognized by many gardeners for their positive effect in aiding overall plant health. Seaweed includes trace elements and micronutrients and helps to increase chlorophyll production in plants. Certain seaweed-based products include cytokinins; these are natural growth regulators that act as a growth stimulant for above- and below-ground growth.

Some liquid formulations can be sprayed directly on to plants, whereby the nutrients contained within them are then absorbed through the plant leaves. Other formulations can be dug into the soil.

Soil Improvers

There are also soil improvers based on biostimulants. These are made from plant-based raw materials and are often supplied in a pellet form that is incorporated in the soil or compost. They can help plants with mineralization, allowing plants to absorb more nutrients. These products also stimulate the beneficial microbial life in the soil, particularly around the root zone, helping to restore the natural balance in the soil.

These products can almost be viewed as slow-release organic fertilizers.

An example of when such soil improvers have been utilized successfully can be referenced in how gardeners have restored plant health in box plants and hedges that have been attacked by a combination of box tree moth and box blight, leaving the plants in a very bad way. The application of these products as a top dressing in the soil in the spring and autumn boosts the plants' health, helping them to grow back and become more resilient against future pest and disease attacks.

The expanding use and availability of biostimulant products can help the gardener to increase the overall health of plants, making them stronger and more resilient against pest and disease attack. This is increasingly important with the move away from not only insecticides, but also from fungicides for disease control. Fungicides share many of the problems associated with insecticides, as plant diseases become resistant to them and their impact on the environment is mainly negative.

The use of biostimulants requires some forward thinking, as they are not a curative solution to pest and disease problems, but are about plant husbandry and helping to create the conditions for strong, healthy growth. If biostimulants can help plants to function more efficiently with less reliance on synthetic fertilizers, this can only be good for nature.

Soil boost, a pellet version of a biostimulant that has many applications.

Soil boost acts like an organic slow-release fertilizer.

CONCLUSION

There is certainty some forward momentum, pushing gardeners towards using natural ways of controlling insect pests in their gardens. This is being triggered by a combination of factors.

Most gardeners do want to find natural and environmental solutions to troublesome insect pests, as few enjoy applying chemical insecticides, especially with the concerns widely published in the press about their impact on bees and human health. Some gardeners do still hold the view that insecticides are easier to apply, more effective and cheaper than natural forms of biological pest control. Even gardeners with this mindset, however, are opting for change and natural solutions, owing to the fact that there are very few insecticides left available for gardeners to use, as the majority have been withdrawn from sale. Some insect pests, such as lawn pests, have no chemical insecticides available for use against them. This forces gardeners previously reluctant to a change in method to adapt to using other means of pest control.

Even if there was more choice of insecticides, this form of pest control is still flawed and short-sighted, as insects will always find a way around them. The ability of insects to become resistant to insecticides is well documented; the more an insecticide is used, the greater the percentage of insects that survive. This issue becomes much greater when there are only a few insecticides left to choose from. Insecticides also tend not be specific, so their use impacts other forms of wildlife, which might show as a decline in frog or bee populations. Some researchers are even looking at how insecticides influence insect behaviour, such as the ability of parasitic wasps to find their prey, and how this ability might be reduced with the application of certain insecticides.

Nature has found a way to reduce the effectiveness of insecticides, but at the same time has offered an alternative in the form of insects' natural enemies. This is not a perfect system of pest control and indeed there is not always an obvious natural enemy that can be deployed against a specific insect pest that is causing problems. The use of natural enemies can be constricted by the environment they are being used in. Applications in greenhouses generally remain easier to manage than those outside, although big strides are being made with their use outdoors, especially with the expanding use of nematodes against a wide variety of insect pests.

The frequency of applications of some natural enemies can become quite expensive to the gardener. This is beginning to change, however, as much more choice of biological control is becoming available. This is particularly true for gardeners who shop online, with numerous companies starting to offer these products. This will inevitability lead to the products becoming cheaper to buy.

Biological pest control and the use of natural enemies does require a different approach to that of using insecticides. More planning, monitoring and patience is required. It can take time for the natural enemies to win the battle and sometimes they do not win in time. For many, attempting the use of natural enemies is a learning process, and the more you use, the greater the success rate. Learning to apply these natural enemies can also be fun and interesting; most gardeners and their children will be fascinated by watching these insects and organisms at work.

Nature provides solutions, while also liking to throw in more challenges! This often comes in the form of new pests. Increasing world temperatures and the

Birmingham Botanical Gardens.

movement of people and plants around the globe can result in a wider distribution of some insect pests. In the UK, there is a constant battle to prevent non-native insect pests from establishing, but this is not always possible. The solution is often discovered in finding which natural enemies can be used to counter these new insect pests.

The use of biological control for the gardener is a constantly evolving drive for knowledge of new ways of using the natural enemies of insect pests, but it is surely a better alternative for the environment and humans than relying on harmful man-made insecticides.

BIBLIOGRAPHY

Calvo-Agudo, M. *et al.*, 'Neonicotinoids in Excretion Product of Phloem-Feeding Insects Kill Beneficial Insects', *Proceedings of the National Academy of Sciences* (August 2019, 116(34))

Greenwood, P., Halstead, A. and the Royal Horticultural Society, *Pests and Diseases: The Complete Guide to Preventing, Identifying and Treating Plant Problems* (Dorling Kindersley Ltd, 1997)

Helyer, N., Brown, K. and Cattlin, N.D., *Biological Control in Plant Protection* (Manson Publishing Ltd, 2004)

The Royal Horticultural Society, 'Common Pest Identification Guide', https://www.rhs.org.uk/advice/common-pest-identification-guide [Accessed November 2021]

The Royal Horticultural Society, 'Biological Control in the Home Garden', https://www.rhs.org.uk/advice/profile?PID=506 [Accessed November 2021]

Van der Ent, S. *et al.*, *Knowing and Recognizing: The Biology of Pests, Diseases and their Natural Solutions* (Koppert B.V., 2017)

INDEX

RELATED TITLES FROM CROWOOD

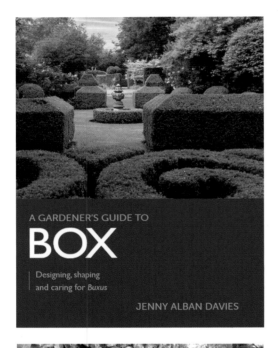

A GARDENER'S GUIDE TO
BOX

Designing, shaping
and caring for *Buxus*

JENNY ALBAN DAVIES

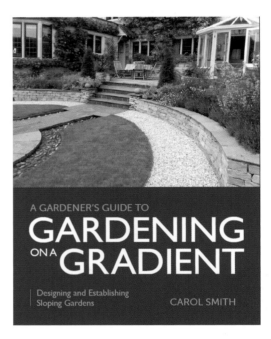

A GARDENER'S GUIDE TO
GARDENING
ON A GRADIENT

Designing and Establishing
Sloping Gardens

CAROL SMITH

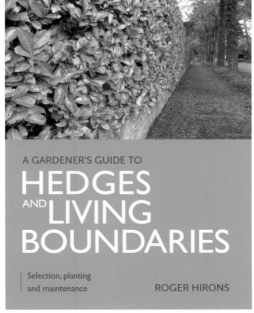

A GARDENER'S GUIDE TO
HEDGES
AND LIVING
BOUNDARIES

Selection, planting
and maintenance

ROGER HIRONS

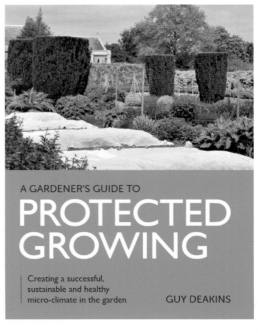

A GARDENER'S GUIDE TO
PROTECTED
GROWING

Creating a successful,
sustainable and healthy
micro-climate in the garden

GUY DEAKINS